¶B The Practitioner's Bookshelf

Hands-On Literacy Books for Classroom Teachers and Administrators

Dorothy S. Strickland, Celia Genishi, and Donna E. Alvermann
LANGUAGE AND LITERACY SERIES EDITORS*

Literacy Essentials for English Language Learners:
Successful Transitions
Maria Uribe and Sally Nathenson-Mejía

Literacy Leadership in Early Childhood:
The Essential Guide
Dorothy S. Strickland and Shannon Riley-Ayers

* For a list of current titles in the Language and Literacy Series, see *www.tcpress.com*

Literacy Essentials for English Language Learners

Successful Transitions

Maria Uribe
Sally Nathenson-Mejía
Foreword by Kathy Escamilla

Teachers College
Columbia University
New York and London

Published by Teachers College Press, 1234 Amsterdam Avenue, New York, NY 10027

Library of Congress Cataloging-in-Publication Data

Uribe, Maria, 1957–
    Literacy essentials for English language learners : successful
        transitions / Maria Uribe, Sally Nathenson-Mejía ; foreword by
        Kathy Escamilla.
        p. cm. — (Language and literacy series. Practitioner's bookshelf)
    Includes bibliographical references and index.
    ISBN 978-0-8077-4904-3 (pbk. : alk. paper)
        1. English language—Study and teaching (Elementary)—
    Foreign speakers. 2. Education, Bilingual—United States.
    3. Multicultural education—United States. I. Nathenson-Mejía,
    Sally, 1951– II. Title.
    PE1128.A2U75 2008
    372.65'21—dc22   2008017958

ISBN 978-0-8077-4904-3 (paper)

Printed on acid-free paper
Manufactured in the United States of America

15 14 13 12 11 10 09 08   8 7 6 5 4 3 2 1

To Enrique, Melissa Adriana, and Gwendolyn Sofia, who taught me what it truly means to be bicultural, bilingual, and biliterate.

Con todo mi amor, snm.

To Mauricio, Liliana, Francisco, Angela, Anmarie, and Madeline, who have been the meaning of my life.

Los quiero mucho, Maria.

Contents

Foreword

GIVEN THE GROWING NUMBER OF English Language Learners (ELLs) in U.S. schools, there is a critical need for books such as *Literacy Essentials for English Language Learners: Successful Transitions*. Teachers, administrators, and other educators need solid information about how to implement effective literacy programs for second language learners in a way that values and supports the languages and cultures of these children. Yet, this essential information has been lacking in official reports on children's literacy. In December 2000, the National Reading Panel (NRP) report was released to the public (National Institute of Child Health and Human Development, 2000). This report identified five research-based elements that it deemed critical to effective approaches to reading instruction for children whose first language *is* English: phonics, phonemic awareness, fluency, vocabulary, and comprehension. The NRP chose not to include scientific literature related to the development of literacy for students who are second (or third, or fourth) language learners of English. Many books and articles have been written on how to utilize the findings of the NRP report to revise and improve reading instruction. Moreover, many commercial publishers of reading programs have revised their materials in response to the NRP's findings. These programs have been implemented nationally, despite their lack of relevant research to one of the fastest growing populations of students in U.S. schools.

In 2006, the *Report of the National Literacy Panel on Language-Minority Children and Youth* was published. The purpose of this research report was to address research findings related to teaching literacy to ELLs, which the NRP had not addressed (August & Shanahan, 2006). Most significant in this report was not what the panel found, but what was missing. The report repeatedly lamented the dearth of scientifically based research on teaching literacy to ELLs. Notably, the NRP included 450 studies in its review, while the National Literacy Panel on Language-Minority Children and Youth included only 107.

The combination of the NRP's exclusive focus on native-English-speaking children, along with the dearth of research on teaching literacy to ELLs, speaks to the critical need for books such as this one. In this book, Maria Uribe and Sally Nathenson-Mejía have done a masterful job of utilizing the research evidence from both the NRP and the National Literacy Panel on Language-Minority Children and Youth reports to create an evidence-based and hands-on guide for developing effective literacy instruction for English Language Learners.

As it sets forth a set of alternative approaches designed to make literacy programs for ELL children more meaningful and effective, the book challenges current conventional wisdom about literacy teaching for second language learners. The authors state that, "Effective teaching for ELL students is more than 'good teaching.' It is providing academic information, strategies, and language in a manner that is step-by-step, explicit, visual, and hands-on, *all at once and all the time*" (emphasis in original). Further, the authors promote literacy teaching that is, "not teaching from formulas, but teaching from informed practice."

The authors acknowledge the value of the five components of effective literacy instruction proposed by the NRP, but suggest that, for ELLs, the order of importance of these components, as well as the emphasis on each of these components, should be different. The authors convincingly argue that meaning (comprehension) must be at the core of the pedagogy of literacy instruction for ELLs, and contend that comprehension be considered "first, last, and continuously." They go on to provide sample lesson plans and structures to demonstrate how comprehension can be at the core of reading instruction for ELLs. Literacy instruction for ELLs should also include a focus on vocabulary, learning to read high-frequency words, phonemic awareness, phonics *in the context of reading texts*, and fluency.

The authors also suggest that a sixth component of effective literacy instruction for ELLs needs to be added: oral language development. It seems obvious that ELLs need to learn to speak English as they are learning to read and write it.

Conventional wisdom has concluded far too often that ELLs have the same needs as native English speakers who are struggling in reading, but the authors demonstrate that ELLs in fact need *different* instruction from struggling native English speakers. They suggest that literacy instruction be strength-based and should begin with what children know (including their native language). Starting from what children know, rather than from a vantage point of perceived needs or deficits, is a wonderful perspective that is woven throughout this book.

Literacy instruction for ELLs must take into account the critical role that cultural knowledge plays in learning to interact with text, and must include the development of *cultural schema* in literacy lessons (which is different than background knowledge). Further, literacy programs for ELLs must consider and use a child's native language (even if English is the sole medium of instruction), and must include explicit teaching of social academic language (the language necessary to collectively cooperate in book talks and work together on literacy and content projects). This book is replete with examples of how literacy instruction must be uniquely tailored to the ELL population, and includes numerous examples that move theory to practice. Moreover, the focus on oral language development and the chapter on writing move the content and import of this book beyond either the NRP or the National Literacy Panel reports.

Written in a clear and reader-friendly manner, this will be a book that is read and re-read by practitioners and quoted often in the literature. It will be used by bilingual/ESL teachers, as well as by monolingual English teachers who have ELLs in their classrooms. Most importantly, it will help ELL children have access to quality literacy instruction. Uribe and Nathenson-Mejía are to be commended for this articulate, intelligent, compassionate, and practical book.

—Kathy Escamilla

REFERENCES

August, D., & Shanahan, T. (Eds.). (2006). *Developing literacy in second language learners: Report of the National Literacy Panel on Language-Minority Children and Youth.* Mahwah, NJ: Erlbaum.

National Institute of Child Health and Human Development. (2000). *Report of the National Reading Panel. Teaching children to read: An evidence-based assessment of the scientific research literature on reading and its implications for instruction. Reports of the subgroup* (NIH Publication No. 00-4754). Washington, DC: U.S. Government Printing Office. Also available at http://www.nichd.nih.gov/publications/nrp/report.htm

Acknowledgments

DURING THE TIME WE HAVE SPENT writing this book we have had wonderful people around us who influenced and inspired us to continue our work and never give up. They have become part of our project and we would like to recognize them.

The first ones are our husbands Mauricio Uribe and Enrique Mejía, who during all this time have given us the support and encouragement to continue and work together for long hours without any hesitation. Without them it would have been impossible to accomplish our job.

Dr. Stephanie Townsend was the first person who read our initial drafts and gave us words of encouragement for our work. We all know that writers need someone who is interested in their work and that person was Stevie.

Dr. Carole Basile gave her time and commitment to our work, which was extremely helpful. The feedback she provided was definitely the inspiration to continue with our journey.

Laurie Grosselfinger, the principal of Goldrick Elementary, gave us words of motivation and also unconditionally gave us the place and the time for writing and talking about our work.

We would like to recognize all the teachers and students from Goldrick who were our inspiration to write this book. They helped us to think about our ideas and strategies of teaching for English Language Learners. We hope their dedication and professionalism help other teachers to realize that teaching comes from our hearts and that there are no limits for learning.

To our Teachers College Press editors, Meg Lemke, Susan Liddicoat, and Karl Nyberg, we would like to express our deepest thanks. Meg gave us the professional support we needed to move forward, Susan did a heroic job of editing that helped us express our ideas in an organized, coherent manner, and Karl helped us put the finishing touches on the manuscript to make this work truly professional. Thank you all.

In addition, we want to thank the most important young people in our lives, our children Liliana, Francisco, Angela, Melissa, and Gwendolyn Sofia, who have always been very proud of us. Along with them, our grandchildren Anmarie, Madeline, and Vahco, who are the best examples of how children can acquire two languages, helped to inspire our work. We hope that all of you feel very proud of what we did and that this book inspires you to fulfill all your dreams.

Finally, it is an honor to have Dr. Kathy Escamilla write the foreword for our book. She not only accepted our request to be part of the book but also inspired us throughout the time it took to produce the book. Thank you.

Literacy Essentials for English Language Learners

Successful Transitions

Introduction

Think about trying to push a basketball through a keyhole. First you have to deflate the ball, then you have to push it down and fold it up tight in order to make it fit. What you end up with doesn't look like a basketball at all since it gets totally mangled as you force it through that little keyhole. The people on the other side may not realize that it even is a basketball, it has been so transformed.

BEING IN AN ENVIRONMENT where many teachers and students do not understand you is a very frustrating experience for students, at any age. When you are first learning a language, trying to get your ideas across is like pushing that basketball through the keyhole. Every day in schools throughout the United States this is the experience of the increasing number of students for whom English is not their first language. From 1995 to 2006, the number of English Language Learners increased by 57.17%. In 1995 there were almost 3.3 million such students, and in 2006, over 5 million (National Clearinghouse for English Language Acquisition and Language Instruction Educational Programs, 2007). Therefore, teaching all subject areas to these students has become one of the challenges for American schools (Capps et al., 2005; Smiley & Salsberry, 2007). The need to pay attention to English Language Learners' cultural and language adaptations to U.S. schools and communities represents a profound shift of beliefs, understandings, and practices on the part of educators across the country (Lachat, 2004).

The purpose of this book is to provide instructional strategies for teachers who are working with English Language Learners in kindergarten through 5th grade. No matter what previous experience students have had with English, and no matter what grade they are in, it is the classroom teachers who have the primary responsibility for moving these students into English literacy. The teachers who will be providing instruction in English may have no knowledge about or little proficiency in the students' native languages. The teachers may be in a location where there are few English Language Learners and thus little English as a Second Language instruction and no native language support. Or the teachers may be new to a school or district that has many English Language Learners, but may lack personal background and experience teaching these students. They may be in a school that provides native language support through 2nd grade, but now the children are in their intermediate English language classroom. Or they might be in a school that has no native language support and expects students to learn as they go in English language classrooms.

Whatever the situation and whatever languages the children already speak, we have written this book to give teachers a greater understanding of the strengths and needs of these students. Our intention is to provide instructional strategies to support the successful literacy development of English Language Learners and to address the concerns teachers face in their classrooms in order to meet national standards in English language arts (National Council of Teachers of English/International Reading Association, 1996).

English Language Learners come from diverse cultural and linguistic backgrounds. The Urban Institute report, *The New Demography of America's Schools* (Capps, Fix, Murray, Ost, Passel, & Herwantoro, 2005) indicates the approximate percentages of the origins of immigrant children in U.S. public schools: 37% from Mexico, 17% from other Latin American and Caribbean countries, 25% from Asia, 4% from Africa, and 17% from Europe, Canada, and Oceania. Because of this distribution, many examples in this book are of students whose primary language is Spanish. However, the instructional strategies can be utilized with all students whose native language is not English.

TERMS AND PERSPECTIVES THROUGHOUT THIS BOOK

We believe it is important at the beginning to explain the terms that will be used in this book and to clarify our positions on teaching English Language Learners.

English Language Learning

There are a variety of terms used to identify people who are not native English speakers: Limited English Proficient (LEP), ESL students or second language learners, Bilingual/Biliterate students, and English Language Learners. We will be using the acronym ELL to refer to "English language learning." We object to the usage that refers to students as "ELLs." It seems to us dehumanizing to refer to children using acronyms, and so we have chosen to use "ELL students" instead.

There are also many different terms used for teaching English to non-native speakers. One of the most common for elementary education is English as a Second Language (ESL). We will use this when we talk about specific instruction for non-native English speakers. Many districts also use English Language Acquisition (ELA) when referring to their curriculum or departments that focus on instruction for non-native English speakers. Another term often used for English instruction is English Language Development (ELD).

Transition

According to the *American Heritage Dictionary of the English Language* (2006), *transition* means "the *process of change*: a process or period in which something undergoes a change and passes from one state, stage, form, or activity to another." Therefore, when students undergo a transition from their native language to English, they are in a living process of adapting to different language, cultural, and academic expectations (Au, 1993; Trueba, 1988). It is important to understand that English Language Learners face the transition process from unique angles, depending on their native language literacy proficiency, English proficiency, time in the United States, and a myriad of other factors.

Language Transition. In this book our focus is *not* "transitional programs," which move ELL students from native language to English instruction after 2 or 3 years. The process of transition we discuss here begins as soon as ELL students enter a school in which the primary language being used is different from the language they speak at home and continues throughout their years in school. Therefore, for us, transition is not one point in time; it does not happen when a student reaches a particular grade. Successful transition requires that the entire school have a specific infrastructure in which all the elements and personnel support ELL children in the changes they are facing. The teachers across grade levels and from all content and enrichment areas ensure that students have the cultural, language, and literacy development that helps them meet the academic standards and succeed as new participants in the school.

Literacy Transition. When we discuss transition in literacy, it is not about learning to read and write in a first language and then learning to read and write in another language. Native language literacy experiences at home—such as reading native language newspapers; writing grocery lists, mail, and email, native language worship—provide a foundation for literacy. Thus, we are looking at a simultaneous understanding and acquisition of literacy in the two languages ELL students have, whether or not the school provides native language instruction. Literacy transition takes place over time as students acquire increasingly more vocabulary and skills that increase their proficiency in English. In this book we have adapted familiar literacy strategies and routines and in some cases restructured them to help students identify the similarities and differences between their native language and English.

Bilingualism and Biliteracy

It is our belief that all students who come to school with a native language that is not English are deserving and capable of keeping their native language while learning English. This may or may not happen through the efforts of the school's program, but our experience has taught us that it is possible. Our hope is that students who learn English as their second or third language in school will become fully bilingual and biliterate.

IMPORTANT INSTRUCTIONAL STRATEGIES TO SUPPORT TRANSITION

Throughout the book we will use the terms *build on, explain,* and *involve* to signal the kinds of instruction teachers can use to help ELL students in the transition to English.

- *Build on* refers to students' background knowledge. It is essential to find out what students know about a topic and use that information as a point of reference (Moje et al., 2004; Peregoy & Boyle, 2008; Short & Fitzsimmons, 2007). Teachers *build on* the prior knowledge of students by using what students know to introduce English vocabulary, enhance their conceptual understandings, and move them forward toward new knowledge and understandings.

- *Explain* refers to explicit instruction (Chamot & O'Malley, 1996; Flynn & Hill, 2006; Peregoy & Boyle, 2008). When teachers *explain*, they give specific descriptions of what is being talking about, how it connects to students' background knowledge, and how the information can be used by students.
- *Involve* refers to interactive instructional techniques that help students remember and apply the information being taught (Cambourne, 1995; Miller, 2002; Peregoy & Boyle, 2008). Actively involving students helps them engage with the topic and material in ways that are meaningful and memorable.

These strategies are all part of good teaching instruction; however, when teaching native English speakers, we often don't pay explicit attention or give significant time to *all three*. With ELL students, it is imperative that teachers take the time to engage deliberately in each step so that students will not become lost in the instructional process. Effective teaching for ELL students is more than "good teaching." It is providing academic information, strategies, *and* language in a manner that is step-by-step, explicit, visual, and hands-on, *all at once and all the time*.

OVERVIEW OF THIS BOOK

The following chapters will address each of the literacy curriculum aspects that should be incorporated during instruction for ELL students in order to help them undergo a successful and cohesive process of transition during kindergarten through 5th grade. Chapters 1 and 2 provide information for teachers about the need to access and build on students' background knowledge and how to organize a learning environment that takes their needs into consideration. Chapters 3, 4, and 5 cover the components of comprehensive literacy instruction: read aloud, shared reading, and guided reading. These chapters will consider what direct instruction should look like for various groups of ELL students, by age and language proficiency. Chapter 6 looks at writing instruction and what we can learn from what students already know about written language. The chapters on the literacy components also give ideas about how to assess students' abilities in these areas. At various points in each chapter a feature entitled "What We Know" will highlight information from the professional research literature related to the topic at hand.

Throughout this book our intention is to help teachers address the literacy and language needs of ELL students. We believe in high expectations, and we believe that ELL students need the best teaching techniques to help them attain district and state standards, demonstrate high levels of performance on state assessments, and most important, enjoy success in life. We firmly believe that ELL students can achieve the same levels of proficiency as native English speakers if all the school infrastructures, methods, techniques, and expectations undertake to support this achievement.

Schools must put into place a strategic system that helps ELL students build on what they know, continually moving forward in both language and literacy acquisition. For example, ELL kindergartners should be exposed to fun and meaningful language and literacy activities in English in ways that are designed specifically for them to develop language and acquire literacy. In 1st grade they will continue to develop English language, literacy, and content concepts, with more opportunities to apply this knowledge through reading and writing.

Having been exposed to structured, systematic language and literacy acquisition since kindergarten, ELL 2nd graders know that they will be able to learn new academic concepts and ideas, and will have many opportunities to apply their knowledge in English. They will not be surprised or intimidated by the increased use of academic English because they will have grown confident in their abilities to acquire and use the language. In 3rd through 5th grades, ELL students are prepared to spend more content instruction time in English. This kindergarten-to-5th-grade transition progresses through the years when students' cognitive development moves from concrete to abstract. It takes advantage of what ELL students know and can do at every grade level and makes moving into English instruction a natural part of school.

CHAPTER 1

Background Knowledge: Its Role in English Language Learning

ACTIVATING BACKGROUND knowledge for ELL students usually requires more than just asking, "What do you know about . . . ?" when introducing a new concept or a new idea. Many factors play a role when children need to comprehend a text. Children need to decode, know what words mean, and be able to break complex sentences down into parts to be able to understand them. Most important, reading becomes especially difficult when children are not able to comprehend because they are not familiar with a topic. Their experiences may have been very different from what is being presented in their new school environment.

Activating prior knowledge and building new background knowledge for ELL students is a crucial component in literacy development. It is not a matter of just understanding the words or the story; it is a matter of understanding the new world, the traditions and expectations of the culture (Au, 1993). ELL students have particular schemata about what classrooms are, what the teacher's role is, the way teachers are treated, and the way they should interact within the classroom, all based on their previous experiences. For instance, Mexican children, when they come to U.S. schools, most often address teachers by saying "Teacher" (*Maestra*). Many teachers are offended because their names are not used, but taking offense does not help create good relationships and does not teach children what they need to know about U.S. culture. Teachers need to understand, and take the time to explain to the children, that although for them it is a sign of respect to address teachers as "Teacher," in the United States it is a sign of respect to use a title (Mrs., Ms., Mr., Dr.) and last name.

WHAT WE KNOW

When adults think about syntax, we tend to conjure up complex grammar rules and images of diagramming sentences and endless worksheets on sentence structure. Children, however, have what we call "tacit knowledge" about syntax; they just know it, they can't explain it. As infants and toddlers learn their native language, they acquire vocabulary, but they also acquire syntax. This emergent syntax is a continually developing understanding of how to put words together in a particular order, following the patterns and logic of the language spoken by the child's linguistic and cultural community. No one drills toddlers on word order (and if we try, we quickly find it doesn't work), but we do model and reinforce syntax every time we talk with or around them. School-age children have well-developed tacit knowledge of syntax; they know how to use it, but they can't explain it or even identify it. (Nelson, 1998)

Students' lack of background knowledge regarding the mainstream language and culture of the school and the community can make it difficult for ELL students to understand their new world. Wong-Fillmore and Snow (2000) emphasize that readers must apply their linguistic knowledge to the interpretation of texts when they read. This means that readers must make use of the knowledge they possess of their native and new languages (specifically vocabulary and syntax), their schemata about the world, *and* their prior experiences in reading. The difficulty for ELL students is that those experiences that have helped them develop language knowledge and schemata of the world are usually very different from mainstream U.S. cultures and school communities. Their tacit knowledge of syntax may be of no help in understanding English, their schemata about school culture may not help them interpret school environments in the United States, and their English vocabulary may be limited or nonexistent. Therefore, even if they have been in the United States for 3 or 4 years, teachers cannot simply presuppose that ELL readers will be able to directly apply their background knowledge about language and the world to interpret the texts they are confronted with and draw conclusions in the same way native English speakers do.

In this chapter we will demonstrate how background knowledge affects what learners understand and how important it is for teachers to gather information about ELL students' educational histories and academic knowledge as well as what they know about school culture. We also will provide examples of literacy instruction that *builds on* what ELL students do know, that *explains* more about how English works, and *involves* ELL students actively in the learning process.

EXPERIMENTING WITH BACKGROUND KNOWLEDGE: A SELF-TEST

To give you a feel for how background knowledge influences learning, we'd like you to try an activity that is very similar in format to those given to elementary school students. Reading a short passage, and answering questions about it, is common in reading programs, standardized tests, and statewide assessments. Have a go with these.

> *After getting into town late last night, I was suffering real jet lag from crossing several time zones and an ocean. I'd been away for long enough that I'd lost track of not only time, but what day it was. Sure that a walk would clear my head, I decided to take a stroll and get some coffee.*
>
> *I walked the three blocks to my favorite coffee place, and on the way I noticed there were more flags out than usual. Arriving at the neighborhood shopping area I saw many red, white, and blue banners and several street vendors selling food from their outdoor grills. I looked at my watch and realized it was almost noon, and the wonderful smells coming from the grills made my mouth water. I was hungry! I bought lunch and sat on a bench to eat and look around.*
>
> *Several announcements were posted on store windows urging people to attend different fireworks and music shows. It dawned on me that all these festivities were for that night, so I called my friend and made plans to meet at the lake for an evening of fun.*

You unquestionably understood all the words in this selection. Now see how well you can answer the multiple-choice questions below.

1. Why were the colors on the banners significant?
   A. These colors announce "caution, construction going on."
   B. These colors are bright and cheery.
   C. These are traditional U.S. colors.
2. What foods were the vendors grilling?

        A. Eggplants and garlic
        B. Hot dogs and hamburgers
        C. Shark and tuna steaks
3. Why would the narrator decide to go to the lake for the evening?
        A. It was a nice day for a swim.
        B. Fishing is always best in the evening.
        C. Fireworks shows are often done by a large body of water.
4. What was the reason for all the festivities?
        A. New Years
        B. Arbor day
        C. 4th of July

Certainly this was not a difficult passage and you were able to visualize the scene easily. Most likely you were able to figure out what day it was before you finished the passage. Now, try reading and answering questions for the next passage.

One Saturday afternoon I decided to take a walk downtown to go out to eat and to people watch. Going toward the town, I saw a bus full of coffee beans and people. When I got there, I saw a house on the corner with traditional decorations on the walls and on the porch. It also had native flowers. When I arrived downtown, I realized I had forgotten that it was a very special day for native coffee workers. It was the traditional parade for the beginning of the year. I was excited because I was going to see the dancers with their traditional dresses, the people selling different kinds of foods, and the church on the corner ringing the bells. I stopped in the most popular restaurant and asked for the bean tray. It was delicious!! I heard the music and saw the natural smiles from everybody. I had a very good time, and I was glad I decided to take a walk that day.

First, ask yourself if there are any words that you don't understand from this text. We are confident that you know the meaning of all the words; but let's see if you can answer the following questions:

1. What color do you think the dancers' dresses were?
        A. Many different colors
        B. Green, white, and red
        C. Yellow, green, and red
2. What kinds of flowers did the house have?

    A. Lilies, roses
    B. Carnations, roses
    C. Geraniums, lilies
3. When is the "beginning of the year" for coffee growers?
    A. January
    B. May
    C. August
4. What did the writer eat for lunch?
    A. Beans, tortillas, and rice
    B. Beans, pork, and eggs
    C. Beans, pork, and tortillas

Most likely the answers you gave will vary according to your own background knowledge. Some of you have traveled and have seen the coffee region in Colombia, so it will be very easy to answer the questions. Some of you have traveled to Mexico, and it will be very easy to generalize the information from your background knowledge. But others will have a great amount of difficulty answering the questions because you have no background knowledge about Colombia or Latin America. Of course, knowing that the story takes place in Colombia is a piece of information that is essential to truly understand the story. If you know where the story takes place, whether in Colombia, México, Ethiopia, or Indonesia—all coffee-growing countries with their own traditions—you will have an easier time visualizing the events in the story. Very often we forget to make explicit for ELL students those essential details that may help comprehension.

Surely you want to know the answers to our second quiz. For question number 1 it is C, because those are the traditional colors of the region where coffee grows in Colombia. Question number 2 is C also; even though Colombia does grow roses and carnations, the particular town that had the fiesta is not in the region for those flowers because of the cooler temperature. If you know why coffee is grown in certain regions, you will know these details. For question number 3, the answer is A, January, because that is when the *Feria del Café* is held. And for question number 4, the answer is B because in Colombia people do not eat tortillas, which are considered a foreign food.

These examples show how students with a language and culture different from U.S. schools come with many rich experiences.

However, these experiences are different from those expected in the texts that they read and the school environment in their new country. The examples in this chapter will help teachers to see how to plan their lessons in order to take advantage of students' existing background knowledge and how to use those experiences to build more background knowledge.

BACKGROUND KNOWLEDGE OF SCHOOL ENVIRONMENTS

Many countries have different kinds of educational settings and ways of instructing. Children who come from Spanish-speaking countries often come from classrooms of 35, 40, and sometimes more than 60 children. They cannot interact very much with the teachers or have cooperative learning due to the numbers of children in the classroom. The teachers use a very specific teaching approach in which every student is part of the whole-class instruction without too many choices. In Mexico children work from textbooks provided by the federal government. Every child in Grades 1–6 has the same book and works on the same unit during the same week of the year. Children all over Mexico wear uniforms to school. They learn to read and write in 1st grade, many without the benefit of preschool or kindergarten. They learn their multiplication tables a year before many children in the United States, without the support of manipulatives. For the most part, in Mexico, children do not sit at group tables, engage in literature circles, have independent reading time, or create group projects.

In Vietnam children go to school 6 days a week, Monday through Saturday. The school day is about 4 hours long. They also are taught traditional manners and customs, including social skills and respect for their elders, family, and community. Most school days begin with a test. The teacher calls on students to stand and answer a question. Students sit together and chant during lessons. Saturday is a review day. Students stand and tell the teacher what they have learned during the week. Students do not get grades on a report card. Instead, they are ranked first, second, third, and so on. In some schools students must wear uniforms to school. Many schools are overcrowded. Most schools have no playground equipment or extra activities. Students take turns cleaning their school.

They are divided into clean-up groups. On their assigned day, they come to school early to sweep rooms, clean chalkboards, and empty the trash. Some children, especially in rural areas, do not go to school because they must work to help their families afford basic needs (Taverna & Hongell, 2005).

Build on. These examples show how new students may be overwhelmed when they arrive in a U.S. classroom where the children are used to choices, table seating, independent work, and questioning the teacher. Sometimes children may exhibit discipline problems or become very quiet; in either case they often aren't able to learn well in the new environment without some help and time to adjust. Consequently, teachers need to find out what school situations ELL students come from, and *build on* that schema to introduce the new setting in which the students are going to learn, making it comprehensible and familiar for them. Just the act of helping students describe and compare school situations lets them know they are valued and recognized and helps them become familiar with and more comfortable in their new environment.

Communicating with students who speak no English, or very little English, poses particular challenges for teachers who do not speak the students' language. We encourage teachers to facilitate communication through the use of pictures, by using student buddies who do speak the students' language, and by enlisting the aid of paraprofessionals and/or school parents who speak the language.

Explain and Involve. When children come to the classroom, it is worth taking the time to *explain* the specifics of the school, the routines and the children's responsibilities, as well as the terminology teachers use to communicate all of this. The environment of the school is a key component in the success of the child (Pérez & Torres-Guzmán, 2002). Teachers need to take the time to show and discuss various aspects of school, including the physical setup, groupings, cooperative work, independent work, materials, and the expectations surrounding each one. Here again, it is important for teachers who do not speak the students' language to get help from others who do—fellow students, older students, paraprofessionals, parents, or community members. Even a brief orientation in a student's native language will help him or her acclimate more quickly and feel more comfortable in the new environment.

Typically in U.S. elementary schools, students have access to the halls, student bathrooms, other classrooms, lunch room, library, and office with general permission ("Grab a hall pass!") during school hours. However, students do not have access to the principal's office, teachers' lounge, kitchens, supply closets, and other places without very specific permission or without being accompanied by an adult. These "rules" may not be written down or directly explained so students new to the school will have no idea that the rules even exist.

The same is often true with regard to homework, use of classroom materials, use of classroom time, and so on. Taking the time to make sure new students are familiar with their surroundings, the expectations of the school, and the terminology associated with all of this, will help students to relax, feel more confident in their new environment, and be prepared to learn.

In addition, mainstream U.S. teachers tend to use a question format when actually ordering a student to do something, such as, "Would you please get off the table and sit on your chair?" This sounds like a request, but in fact is an order, not to be refused. Teachers also ask, "Do you think you made a good choice of whom to work with?" It would be very easy for the student to say "Yes," if he did not know that the teacher really meant, "You did *not* make a good choice; change partners." These are simultaneously linguistic and cultural aspects of English and school that students may not understand without explicit explanations.

Teachers should be very explicit about how school English works, what specific words and phrases mean (such as, "Grab a hall pass!"), and how to find information students need in order to complete their work (if it's in the "LMC" [Library Media Center], what does LMC mean, where is it found, and how does one find something in there?). These are all details that those of us who have grown up in U.S. communities and schools take for granted. It is not enough to just tell ELL students something; teachers must show what they mean and show how to do it. This is a delicate balancing act. It is very important to us that teachers *never* make ELL students feel stupid, and it is easy to feel that way when one is in an incomprehensible situation. At the same time, teachers should know that there are subtleties in the English language and in school expectations that make it difficult for ELL students to understand and succeed; therefore, some very explicit, basic teaching is required, even

> ### WHAT WE KNOW
>
> Activating background knowledge is one of the basic strategies in children's literacy. In order for students to understand what they read and write, they need to have prior knowledge that helps them connect to the text (Echevarria & Graves, 2003; Echevarria, Vogt, & Short., 2004; Escamilla, 1993; Keene & Zimmermann, 2007; Kendal & Khuon, 2005).

if a student is 10 or 12 years old. We will try to give examples of *explain* and *involve* that are specific without being demeaning to ELL students, that help them understand the information and content, but do not make them feel they are not smart and capable.

BACKGROUND KNOWLEDGE IN READING

When introducing a text to students, teachers need to help them become familiar with the necessary concepts to understand and make connections to that text. Teachers also need to identify how students relate to the concepts, since children from varied backgrounds will have different interpretations of what is being communicated.

Let's take the example that Escamilla (1993) has used. She asked a group of Caucasian children what a *barrio* is; the children answered that it is where bad people live and there are drugs. Then she asked a group of Latino children what a *barrio* is, and they said it is where their family, their relatives, and their friends live. Neither group was right or wrong; their background knowledge was simply different.

If we think about that example, we can see how confused the children could be if they read about a subject for which they had different background from the teacher. Remember the quiz about the festival in Colombia? Readers who come from different coffee-growing countries will have different responses to the questions.

Build on. As they begin to read a text to or with ELL students, teachers need to draw out from students what they know about the topic and then use that knowledge to *build on* while introducing and reading through the book. This will demonstrate to students that

1. Their teacher values the knowledge and experiences they already have.
2. They can use their knowledge to make connections between their lives and the stories/texts they are exposed to.
3. They can begin to look at texts from new perspectives (e.g., how students from other countries view the text, how U.S. students view the text).

The time teachers take to identify and use students' background knowledge will pay off in making the literacy experience more comprehensible, thus increasing students' learning. (See Table 1.1 for a guide to assessing students' background knowledge.)

Explain and Involve. Once the teacher has identified the ELL students' background knowledge, she or he can start to *explain* and *involve* students in the new concepts, making explicit the differences between and similarities with what the children already know and getting them involved in active responses through talk, acting, drawing, singing, and other activities.

READING LESSON EXAMPLES FOR K–2 ELL STUDENTS

School life is a topic that can be used to get to know students, provide them with useful English language, and help them expand their knowledge of the world and U.S. schools. *This Is the Way We Go to School* by Edith Baer (1990) shows how children from different countries get to school. Some walk through forests, some walk on

TABLE 1.1. Background Knowledge and Experiences

Behaviors	No Evidence	Sometimes	Often
Demonstrates experience in a topic from the text			
Talks about the topic with expression and self-assurance			
Gives examples from the lesson			
Makes connections with the text			
Predicts based on past experiences			
Compares and contrasts his/her experiences with the text			

streets, some ride bikes, take the bus, or get rides in cars. The text is simple and the illustrations are explicit. It is easy to walk through the book and talk about what the characters are doing, giving students English language they can use to share their own experiences.

We have included below a 5-day set of activities for shared reading that teachers can do using this book. The activities can be used to introduce the English language to new speakers or to review language with children who speak some English and perhaps are returning to school after summer break.

You may not need the full 5 days if students are picking up the concepts and vocabulary quickly. Remember to pay attention to the needs of your students. If they are learning quickly, getting bored, or having a difficult time with the content, change your plan to meet their needs. It is important, however, to carry a topic over at least 2 days in order to reinforce concepts and vocabulary before moving on.

You can change the book you are using, while keeping the topic the same. In fact, it is sometimes helpful to have a variety of books on the topic available so you can refer to the different photographs or illustrations to help get ideas across. When working with ELL students, it is also important to have *realia* at hand.

Realia are real or lifelike replicas of items you'll be talking about during lessons. Realistic small toys make great realia. Toy cars, buses, bikes, and people look enough like their counterparts to stand in for the real thing. You'll probably need to use photographs for buildings such as schools, different kinds of houses, hospitals, parks, and so on. Real food items are best, but plastic or wax food will work if they look real.

Lesson for New Speakers of English

Day One: Build on. Read/talk through the book *This Is the Way We Go to School*, making sure students know what *school* is and helping them make connections between the illustrations of walking, bikes, buses, and so on, and the English words.

1. Have available several small toy bikes, cars, school buses, and city buses, and various people of different colors.
2. Using a generic toy school building as your destination and using the toy vehicles, show students how *you* get to school.

3. Have the children choose the mode of transportation they use to get to school and demonstrate going from their house to school.

Day Two: Explain and Involve.

1. Do a quick review of the book's illustrations, focusing on the different school buildings shown.
2. Do a quick review of the modes of transportation, having the students pick up and identify them. Remind students, using the toys, how you get to school now.
3. Show students a picture of yourself as a child. Show them a photo or draw for them a picture of the school you went to then. Show them how you got to school when you were a child.
4. Ask them to draw a picture of the school they went to *before* coming to the United States. Give students 4 x 8 paper so you can use these pictures later to create a group book. If they were not in school, have them draw a picture of their home or community gathering place.
5. Have students place their pictures on the table or floor; have them choose a toy model of the mode of transportation they used then and act out how they got to school. While they are doing this, talk with them about what they are doing, use the language you have been exposing them to (school, bus, car, bike, walk, etc.), and encourage them to use it too.
6. Involve the students as you write a sentence on chart paper for each child. Keep the format of each sentence as similar as possible: "Marta rode to school on a city bus. Keiko rode to school on a bike. Alexi walked to school."

Day Three: Explain and Involve.

1. Review the sentences you wrote on Day Two, reading each one.
2. Involve the students in talking about the school buildings. Look through the students' pictures and involve the students in talking about what they see: size, doors, windows, brick, wood, metal (having real examples, realia, or photos of these items will help). Write down the vocabulary and place the words as labels next to the realia or photos.

3. Hold the students' pictures up one at a time and involve the students as you write one or two sentences about each one. Keep the format of the sentences as similar as possible: "Marta's school is small and made of wood. It has one door and four windows. Keiko's school is big and made of brick. It has two doors and many windows."
4. Go back to the book and look at the illustrations of the schools, using the language you've just been practicing to describe the schools in the illustrations. Involve the students in using the language as much as they are able.

Day Four: Involve.

1. Type all the sentences and print them out so that the description of how they got to school ("Marta rode to school on a city bus.") and the description of the school ("Marta's school is small and made of wood. It has one door and four windows.") are each on separate pieces of paper.
2. Review *This Is the Way We Go to School*.
3. Mix up the sentences about going to school and have students find their own. If needed, help them do this by identifying their names. Read through them all together. Ask students to draw a picture of themselves going to school before they came to the United States.
4. Provide materials for the students to glue their picture and their sentence on a large piece of heavy paper.
5. Repeat with the pictures and sentences about the schools.
6. Use the students' work to make a group book.

Day Five: Involve.

1. Read *This Is the Way We Go to School* to/with the students.
2. Read the group's book with the students and decide on a title. Write the title on the front.
3. Share the group book with various classes and school personnel.

These activities help to solidify the concept of going to school and provide language to help students talk about getting to school and what the school itself looks like. The activities also validate the students' own experiences with school both in the present and before they came to the United States. You also have begun to work on the idea of comparing and contrasting experiences, their own and one another's.

Following these activities you can begin to work on concepts and vocabulary related to the inside of school: what it looks like, what activities they do, what their daily schedule is like. Remember to start with what they already know—what their experiences were like before they came to the United States.

Lesson for Early Intermediate Speakers of English

When working with students who have some command of English, *This Is the Way We Go to School* can be used as a review of ideas and vocabulary to help them remember and practice expressing their ideas about school. They may already have the basic vocabulary covered in Days One to Five for new speakers, in which case the discussion can proceed quickly to the more in-depth comparison of school life across countries and cultures. Students who have more command of English also can discuss the different academic content of their former and current schools, instructional styles and materials, and even their opinions about these different school environments. It is imperative that students engage in higher level thinking and learn to express these ideas. Using the familiar topic of school gives them a safe way to experiment with these ideas and language.

Compare and contrast is a skill that students need in order to achieve standards (Marzano, Pickering, & Pollock, 2004). Teachers can help students compare and contrast what school life is like now with what it was like for each of them before, in ways that value everyone's experiences. Remember to use visuals and manipulatives and ask concrete questions. Here are a few ideas for follow-up lessons that will expand students' background knowledge and reinforce vocabulary and concepts they learned in the lesson.

1. *School day schedule.* Some countries have early (8 a.m. to 2 p.m.) and late (3 p.m. to 9 p.m.) school schedules.
    *   Using two teaching clocks, hold up one that is set to the time of day your school begins. Confirm with the group that this is the time school starts for them now. Hold up another clock and ask, "What time of day did you begin school before?" Change the clock to the various times as you give them a complete sentence, "Marta started school

at 8:30 in the morning. Kayla started school at 1:30 in the afternoon."

2. *School week schedule.* In some countries students attend school 6 days a week. Their day off may depend on the major religious Sabbath day.
   - Using a calendar, confirm with the students the days of the week they attend school now. Ask them, "How many days a week did you go to school before? Which days?" Recite with them the various days as you give them a complete sentence, "Marta attended school Monday through Saturday. Kayla attended school Sunday through Thursday."

3. *School size and classroom arrangement.* Schools have different numbers of students and different classroom configurations.
   - Confirm with the group how many students there are in their classes now. Have students estimate how many were in their classes before they came to the United States. Or show them photos of different class configurations and sizes and have the students choose the ones that are closest to their former school. Some students will come from classes of 50–60, and some may have had only 5 or 10. Discuss the differences, why they exist, and what it was like to be in a large class or very small class compared with now.
   - Some schools have rows of desks, some have tables, some have no furniture and students sit on the floor. Ask students, "How do you sit in class in this school? How did you sit in class in your other school? Who decided where you would sit? What do you like about the way we sit here? What don't you like about it?"

As you ask these questions, it becomes clear that everyone has different experiences and you, as the teacher, are not judging those experiences or elevating the U.S. experience as superior. Instead, you are helping them to recognize concepts that transfer from one language/culture to another and to learn to describe their lives and express their ideas using this new language.

Some of these activities may seem basic. However, it is important to review these concepts with students even if they have been in the U.S. school system for 2, 3, or 4 years. Every year children's conceptual development advances, and they are able to take on more sophisticated vocabulary and grammar structures. By reviewing these basic concepts, using more sophisticated support literature every year, teachers can scaffold students as they learn to use a wider range of vocabulary in talking/writing about their ideas at a higher level.

LANGUAGE LESSON EXAMPLES FOR GRADES 3–5 ELL STUDENTS

Lesson for New Speakers of English

The concept of *homes* can be used to assess and *build on* what ELL students know and then to *explain* and *involve* by giving them English vocabulary to talk about this familiar topic. They can expand their knowledge of various types and styles of homes across cultures and in the United States. Simple comparison charts can be generated with the students to describe the various homes that they lived in before arriving in the United States (see Table 1.2) and the various homes they have lived in since being in the United States (see Table 1.3).

Now the teacher has information upon which to build language and concepts, to talk about what activities are done in which rooms (cooking, eating, sleeping, reading/homework, brushing teeth, washing clothes, playing, etc.), and to use when introducing books. Using photos from magazines and children's drawings, a picture chart can be created and labeled that shows the different houses, what rooms they have, what activities are done in those rooms, and

TABLE 1.2. Homes We Lived in Outside of the United States: China, Mexico, Croatia, Somalia

Home Type	Number and Type of Rooms	Bathroom	Kitchen
Farm house	2; living, sleeping	Outside	Outside
Farm house	4; living, sleeping, kitchen	Outside	Inside
Apartment	3; kitchen, living, sleeping	Inside	Inside
Apartment	2; sleeping	Outside	Outside
City house	3; kitchen, living, sleeping	Outside	Inside
City house	4; kitchen, living, sleeping, working	Inside	Inside

TABLE 1.3. Homes We've Lived in Within the United States

Home Type	Number and Type of Rooms	Bathroom	Kitchen
Farm	1; sleeping	Outside	Outside
Apartment	3; kitchen/living, sleeping	Inside	Inside
Apartment	4; kitchen, living, sleeping	Inside	Inside
City house	4; kitchen, living, sleeping	Inside	Inside
City house	6; kitchen, living, working, sleeping	Inside	Inside

what materials are used. Or a "model" room could be created using cardboard boxes, doll-size furniture, pots, pans, and so forth. The class could begin by comparing kitchens, creating a model of kitchens where students lived outside the United States and kitchens they have now. In creating these models, students' talk will include English vocabulary related to the rooms, furniture, activities, and materials, as well as talk about where to put items, how to label them, and what is similar and different in the various kitchens. All of this talk will enhance and expand students' English vocabulary, expand and reinforce their conceptual knowledge of similarities and differences, and at the same time scaffold their use of English to accomplish tasks and discuss academic topics.

Books with wonderful photos and supportive vocabulary on the topic of homes include the following:

> Amanda Doering's *Homes Around the World ABC* (2005)
> Arthur Dorros's *This Is My House* (1992)
> Dena Freeman's *How People Live* (2003)
> Peter Menzel's *Material World* (1995)
> Ann Morris's *Houses and Homes* (1992)

Lesson About Storytelling Structures

The content of stories is sometimes similar across various countries and cultures, but the structures used in telling the stories often differ across cultures. It is worth spending time to find out students' stories and identify their storytelling structures based on their native languages and cultures. Teachers can then *build on* what students already know, taking advantage of their background knowledge, while at the same time demonstrating respect for their culture and what they know. Mainstream storytelling in the United States tends to be straightforward, moving from the beginning, through to the problem, then resolution and ending. But not every culture, even in the United States, uses this storytelling structure. Latino teachers often talk about how their own families tell stories "around and around," starting from a different topic altogether, bringing in many different points and details, finally getting to the topic and then going off again. Listening to children tell their own life stories, teachers can begin to identify the storytelling structure the students have grown up with. This information should influence the instruction used to teach ELL students to recognize and comprehend the storytelling structure they will find in U.S. texts.

Creating a storyboard of students' own oral personal narratives can help to *explain* and *involve* by demonstrating the similarities and differences among students' storytelling styles. As a student relates a personal story, take quick notes. Once the student finishes, or at another time, have the student draw sketches in a storyboard graphic organizer to show what he or she said and in what order. As you accumulate these storyboards from various students, you and the students will be able to compare them and verbalize how they are similar to and different from U.S. storytelling structures.

ASSESSING THE EDUCATIONAL HISTORY OF ELL STUDENTS

One final aspect about background knowledge is the students' history. Before talking about children's cognitive level, it is very important for teachers to find out the educational history of their students. Most important is to know the language of instruction the students had in the past. Many times, especially for Spanish-speaking children, the language of instruction varies according to the school's program. Let's look at the educational history of Angela, a Spanish speaker who entered school in the United States with no English. She started kindergarten in a bilingual school and received most of her instruction in Spanish with an ESL component. When she moved to 1st grade, she was in a different school, which did not have bilingual education, so she received only English instruction. By the time she went to 2nd grade, the family had moved back to the previous school and the teacher decided to put her in a Spanish class because she was not able to read in either language. By 3rd grade she was assessed as having a possible learning disability and was placed in a bilingual classroom with time in the special education classroom, where the instruction was in English. This lack of consistent instruction from kindergarten to 3rd grade resulted in a lack of academic language development in either Spanish or English.

Unfortunately, we see many cases similar to Angela's— inconsistent language instruction that does not develop a child's language or academic skills. Perhaps this happens because the school does not have the resources to provide consistent instruction across grades, or because the child changes schools often, and the teachers at the new schools do not have access to the history of the child's previous instruction. Along with previous language instruction, teachers need to explore the child's attendance history and the country in which the child was receiving education. Many times children move back and forth between the United States and another country, sometimes within the same year; therefore, the language, style, and content of instruction are different from year to year or even within the same year.

Finding out about a child's instructional history is more than a requirement; it is a necessity in order to provide the best educational experience possible for each child. Acquiring this information is time-consuming and may necessitate home visits to gain enough family trust so that they will share the information. However, the time teachers take to establish these relationships and gather pertinent information about the children will pay off in improved instruction, greater family involvement, and increased engagement by the students (González, Moll, & Amanti, 2005).

SUMMARY

Background knowledge is an essential aspect of students' reading success (Echevarria & Graves, 2003; Escamilla, 1993; Keene & Zimmermann, 2007; Kendal & Khuon, 2005). Teachers need to gather information about their students' educational histories, what they know about school cultures, and what they know academically.

This information will give teachers the foundation to build a comprehensible curriculum for their ELL students.

Once teachers have this information, they can begin instruction with known concepts and provide students with the English to talk about these familiar concepts. We recommend a spiraling sequence that begins with known concepts, uses that knowledge to teach new language, then uses this new, but now familiar, language to move into new concepts (that still *build on* known concepts), and continues on, constantly *building on* what has come before. As teachers move through this spiraling cycle, they should always take into consideration and give value to what ELL students already know about how the world works: daily life, school, city, farm, family, food, and so forth. This background knowledge is essential to help students understand the texts to be read.

CHAPTER 2

Instructional Environment: Creating Support for Learning Language

MANY RESEARCHERS HAVE written descriptions of warm and inviting classrooms to inspire us and demonstrate how effective instruction and learning can take place in a supportive and nurturing environment. Regarding the physical environment, it is important to provide a wealth of literacy materials and easy access to these materials in order to immerse students in reading and writing. Our focus in this chapter, however, is on curriculum planning, grouping for instruction, and the classroom schedule—all integral aspects of the environment that we would like teachers to keep in mind for English Language Learners.

In designing classroom environments for English Language Learners, teachers cannot lose sight of the fact that students are learning both a new language and literacy at the same time. Thus the curriculum design, scheduling, and independent and group time should include conditions that allow students to develop *language* while at the same time developing their reading and writing skills. This chapter will give the reader ideas on how to make connections across the curriculum that will reinforce learning, focus instruction on some of the specifics of academic language and literacy development, and organize the schedule around read alouds, shared reading, guided reading, and independent reading—in both classrooms that do not provide native language instruction and those that do.

CURRICULUM PLANNING FOR READING AND WRITING

Making Connections Across the Curriculum

The first aspect to consider is the curriculum planning done for reading and writing. For ELL students, making connections across instructional areas is essential to develop both language and literacy. We can take a lesson here from teachers in the early grades. Very often in the primary levels teachers plan their lessons around a topic or theme, connecting literacy and content instruction through this theme. For example, a teacher may plan a unit about bears. During math students count bears and do story problems about bears. They read books about bears, research bears, do art projects about bears, and write about bears. This approach provides young children with the language and background knowledge they need to become familiar with the topic and concepts. It is important to remember that ELL students need to learn the language and become familiarized with the content in much the same way early learners do. Therefore, in all grades teachers should connect reading and writing with math, science, and social studies content. Calkins (1994) suggests that for primary students it is necessary to directly connect the concepts from reading to writing; they may not do this automatically on their own. In the case of ELL students of any age, teachers need to make these same direct connections—connect the reading comprehension strategies, the content topic students are reading about, and the genre they are writing in to help them develop language, literacy, and content.

Focusing on Language and Literacy Development

Although the use of content topics is important in the language and literacy development of ELL students, there are other considerations teachers must make regarding curriculum. The national and state literacy standards the children need to achieve require more than instruction in content areas. There is academic language specific to literacy that may be difficult to understand, such as use of emotions, author's purpose, conflict/resolution, leads, transitions, and endings. We suggest that ELL students receive specialized language development in both literacy and content areas (math, social studies, science). The topics often lend themselves to be covered in both, creating a natural connection across curricular areas (teaching

---

WHAT WE KNOW

Echevarria and colleagues (2003, 2004) promote teaching language through content instruction; they suggest using the Sheltered Instruction Observation Protocol model for ELL students. Sheltered instruction (SI) provides relief from "the linguistic demands of mainstream instruction" (2003, p. 53), which is often above the comprehension level of ELL students. "In effective SI courses, language and content objectives are systematically woven into the curriculum of one particular subject area" (2004, p. 13).

---

around themes). However, the academic language specific to each area needs to be taught explicitly and during specific times.

We should remember what Halliday (1975) says about language, that children develop language by "learning the language, learning through language, and learning about language" (as cited in Gibbons, 2002, p. 118). When we look at a common organization of the literacy block, we can find those three components (see Figure 2.1). The read alouds help children learn the language; the children learn through language during the shared readings, and they learn about language during small-group reading and through writing.

FIGURE 2.1. The Literacy Block Cycle

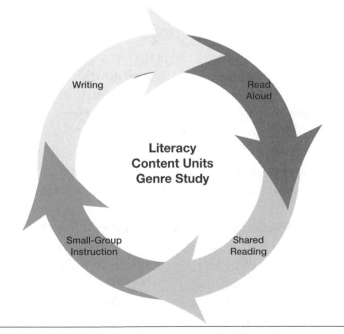

This is exactly what we meant in Chapter 1 when we talked about spiraling instruction for students, instruction that *builds on* itself. For example, when teachers focus on poetry, they plan for children to learn the language of poetry during read alouds, they use poetry as a vehicle for learning the language and its configuration during shared reading, and during the small-group reading and writing children learn about the language used in poetry and how to use it. We can only imagine all the language and content the children can learn, within the same genre, if teachers plan their curricula in a way that continually reinforces the concepts being learned.

GROUPING STUDENTS FOR INSTRUCTION BY LANGUAGE PROFICIENCY

Hand in hand with curriculum decisions are the decisions teachers make about grouping their students in order to ensure that they get the specific instruction and support they need. We believe that during literacy instruction the most effective way to group students is according to language proficiency (how well they understand and speak English). Grouping according to language proficiency allows teachers to provide targeted language instruction, even though children in the group may be at different reading levels. When ELL students are in groups with others at the same language level of English, they are more relaxed and feel more comfortable, which helps them take risks in their second language. Chapter 5 will discuss small-group reading instruction in more depth, including how to provide instruction for a group with different reading abilities but similar English language proficiencies. In this chapter on classroom environment, we want to provide information to help teachers understand how to group students throughout the day—during literacy; during math, social studies, and science; and during other subjects that complement the instructional day.

Many times schools try to group students with similar language proficiency but very different age levels, say, 1st through 4th graders or 2nd through 5th graders. We believe strongly that this is counterproductive for the students. Research in cognitive development (Piaget & Inhelder, 1969), language development (Halliday, 1975; Vygotsky, 1986), reading development (Weaver, 2002) and writing development (Calkins, 1994) has shown that 1st and 2nd graders do not have the same social and academic needs as 3rd, 4th, and 5th graders. In order for teachers to provide appropriate language and literacy instruction, students should be in close age-level groupings. We are not against multiage classrooms, but we have seen that too wide a spread is not effective for teaching language and literacy to English Language Learners.

The following points are important to consider as teachers create literacy groups according to language proficiency:

- At grade levels, teachers create literacy groups for reading instruction across classrooms, according to language proficiencies. It is important to make sure that the teachers with the most experience working with ELL students will have the students with the least amount of English.
- If grouping for literacy across grade-level classrooms is not possible, then teachers will have both ELL students and native English speakers in their class. In this case, make sure the ELL students are in separate small groups, even those students who are more proficient in English. ELL students need different instruction from native English speakers, even those who may be students who are struggling in reading.
- When grouping students by language proficiency, it is vital to build content language and have a specific time to provide English instruction related to content subjects, in order to build background knowledge and language comprehension.

When the school is able to provide this multileveled language grouping arrangement, it allows ELL students opportunities to develop language and literacy with instruction geared toward their specific needs. In addition, during whole-class content instruction they will have opportunities to interact with English-speaking children, who will serve as language models. In this way, all students will learn to appreciate and value the different cultures and learn from them, a most important aspect of education.

SCHEDULING THE LITERACY BLOCK IN K–5 CLASSROOMS

How a classroom's daily schedule is organized, and how this organization provides both access and time to use the materials and supports needed to reach instructional goals, sends a message to children about what is important. For example, many balanced literacy schedules provide large blocks of time in which to work, reflect, and consult. In addition, the materials in the room and their placement, such as easily accessible bookshelves and reading and writing corners, are designed to support students as they become strategic readers and writers.

Typical literacy blocks are scheduled around reading, writing, and skills. In this section we first suggest how this time might be organized to give ELL students the optimum environment for learning. Then we will show how the schedule can be modified to include native language instruction.

The schedule that we propose helps ELL students acquire the English language and at the same time become readers and writers. The times we include are our suggestions for getting the most out of each component of the literacy block. We know that teachers will need to adjust these times based on their own school's schedule and requirements.

Literacy Components in Classrooms Without Native Language Instruction

The first component is 30 minutes of read aloud. This read aloud needs to happen *every day*; it is the opportunity for ELL students to be actively engaged in learning the language through teacher demonstration. Chapter 3 goes into this component in much detail.

After the read aloud, the class is divided into small groups of 20-minute rotations. The rotations should continue to *build on* the activities done during read alouds and/or shared reading time so the children have the opportunity to further practice reading and language in structured, small groups with very specific purposes. Remember the spiraling instructional model. One option could include time working with a support person such as a paraeducator, aide, or volunteer. The support person might work with students on spelling, reading high-frequency words, playing bingo or other games with the high-frequency words, having contests, or other activities that the teacher considers useful to reinforce concepts being learned. While the teacher and the support person are working with the small groups, the rest of the students are guided to choose among a variety of independent reading activities such as:

- Writing a summary of or identifying main ideas from a story read previously
- Reading a book either in their native language or in English
- Listening to tapes of a familiar story with the purpose of practicing fluency and pronunciation
- Choosing something from the library such as magazines, books from different genres, poems, informational literature
- Reading the books the teacher read with them during guided reading
- Reading books chosen from those that are at their reading and age-appropriate language level

The activities and time spent in independent work vary according to grade level. Kindergarten children usually spend between 10 and 15 minutes in small-group reading instruction and each rotation. First and second graders usually spend 15 to 20 minutes in their small-group instruction. In 3rd through 5th grade the time depends on the purpose of the small-group instruction, but typically is 20 minutes.

After the small-group instruction, the teacher can provide skills instruction. We suggest that this be done through shared reading. During shared reading the class reads a book, a poem, or another text together, addressing different elements of literacy (see Chapter 4 for more detail). Shared reading is an excellent instructional method for ELL students to acquire English skills because the text can be used to make connections to English grammar and conventions. For example, if the class is reading a big book, say, *The Little Red Hen*, and there are many quotation marks, then part of the lesson will focus on quotation marks. Or, if there are many questions in the book ("Who will help me sow the wheat?"), the teacher can talk about the structure of questions in English. It is possible to teach the use of quotation marks (or questions), plus vocabulary, plus comprehension, all through the meaningful vehicle of shared reading. Chapter 4 gives much more detail about the process and activities for shared reading.

After the skills instruction through shared reading, the students should spend time working on writing. Chapter 6 will cover how writing development and instruction work for ELL students.

The suggested schedule includes 30 minutes of read aloud, 60 minutes of rotations, 30 minutes of shared reading/skills, and 40 minutes of writing (see Table 2.1). We have put shared reading after guided reading for two reasons. First, we want to have ELL students involved in both read aloud and shared reading every day. If they are done one right after the other, students end up sitting for whole-group instruction for 60 minutes. That is too long; they need time to become more active and put their learning into practice. Second, having shared reading after read aloud, guided reading, and rotations allows the teacher to pull together key learnings from the rest of the literacy block. Shared reading is a review and reinforcement of skills and concepts from that day's instruction.

Although it is important to have a strategic structure in place, each ELL student is an individual and will have different needs. In 4th grade a teacher may have ELL students who have been in the school since kindergarten or 1st grade, others who have been in the United States that long but are new to the school, and still others who are completely new to the country and to English. Their individual needs should be taken into account when deciding who is in which group, doing what activity, and for how long.

Literacy Components in Classrooms with Native Language Instruction

We realize that not every school has the resources to provide native language instruction for all their English Language Learners.

TABLE 2.1. Literacy Block Schedule

Literacy Components	Groupings	Minutes
Read aloud	Whole class	30
Rotations	*Small groups:*	
	Guided reading	20
	Independent reading	20
	Paraeducator's station	20
Shared reading/skills	Whole class	30
Writing instruction	Whole class	40
Total time		160 (2 hours, 40 minutes)

WHAT WE KNOW

Many years of research have shown that literacy is best learned first in one's native language (Calderon, 2006; Cummins, 1981; Escamilla, 1993, 1999; Krashen, 1981; Ovando, Collier, & Combs, 2003). This research supports the use of native language literacy instruction to help ELL students learn English and to become proficient in literacy in English.

However, we strongly encourage, we *urge,* schools to find ways to support native language literacy, through volunteers, paraeducators, teacher recruitment, and high school "buddy" programs. The opportunities teachers provide for students to use their native language as they begin the path to bilingualism and biliteracy will pay off in increased comprehension in both languages, increased linguistic flexibility, greatly enhanced vocabulary, and well-developed understanding of concepts in all the content areas. Literacy activities make this possible because vocabulary, concepts, and text can be taught in students' native language, then applied to texts in English. Since students already comprehend the topic from the native language instruction provided, they can transfer their concept knowledge to English activities, even if the text is not exactly the same.

We both have been involved with schools where the language programs move students into English instruction without seeking to eliminate the use of their native language, Spanish. Some of these programs are dual-language, in which native English speakers learn Spanish in the same way, and at the same time, that native Spanish speakers are learning English. But some of these programs would be characterized as transition programs, moving students out of Spanish instruction into English instruction. The successful programs help students see the value of being bilingual and biliterate. They recognize and capitalize on the need English Language Learners have to use their native language in strategic ways.

For schools and classrooms that provide both Spanish and English instruction, we suggest the schedule in Table 2.2. It is important to note that the actual time spent and the language of instruction depend on the child's language acquisition and reading and writing skills. Not all children can follow this schedule; some of them may need more support in Spanish, some of them may have more opportunities during the day to acquire reading and writing skills. The process of transition is not the same for every child and should be adjusted according to the individual student's needs.

SUMMARY

In summary, we suggest that teachers plan language, literacy, and content curriculum in ways that support the language and literacy development of ELL students. In addition, when planning the literacy block, teachers should think about the various balanced literacy components as part of a whole, each component connecting and building from the one before and laying a foundation for the one to come after. In order to make connections across the whole curriculum, teachers can consider what genre and/or content is being taught elsewhere in the curriculum, what comprehension strategies students need, and how writing can be used to connect to the other components and provide consistency and sequence in the ELL students' language development. This approach will prove to be most productive for the students' learning, as every component *builds on* the other components, thus giving ELL students the language tools necessary to learn, understand, and work independently with language.

TABLE 2.2. Literacy Block for ELL K–5 with Native Language Support in Spanish

Literacy Components	GRADES				
	K/1	2	3	4	5
Read aloud *30 minutes*	English and Spanish every day	Every day English and 3 days Spanish at a different time	Every day English and 3 days Spanish at a different time	Every day English; Spanish once a week at a different time (if teacher has the ability)	Every day English; Spanish once a week at a different time (if teacher has the ability)
Guided reading *20 minutes*	Spanish and English (separately every day)	Every day English and 3 days Spanish (could be done by para-educator)	Every day English and 3 days Spanish (could be done by para-educator)	English (with Spanish support when possible)	English (with Spanish support when possible)
Rotations *20 minutes* x 3 = *60 minutes*	2 in Spanish, 1 in English, every day	2 in Spanish, 1 in English, every day	1 in Spanish, 2 in English, every day	English (with Spanish support when possible)	English (with Spanish support when possible)
Writing K–2: *20 minutes* 3–5: *40 minutes*	Spanish	First semester in Spanish and second semester in English	English (with Spanish support when possible)	English (with Spanish support when possible)	English (with Spanish support when possible)
Shared reading/ skills *30 minutes*	Spanish	English	English	English	English
Shared reading/ skills K–1: *20 minutes*	English, incor-porating writing				

CHAPTER 3

Interactive Read Alouds: Hearing Language

READ ALOUD IS ONE OF the essential components of a complete literacy program for English Language Learners and has been defined as "a planned oral reading of a book or print excerpt, usually related to a theme or genre of study. The read aloud can be used to engage the student listener while developing background knowledge, increasing comprehension skills, and fostering critical thinking" (Elementary Science Integration Project, n.d.). Daily read alouds provide myriad opportunities to model the use of reading strategies and develop the building blocks for success in school: language development, vocabulary development, concept development, reading habits, discussions, recognition, and most important, comprehension of the new language and love for reading (Krashen, 2004). When children enter school with little or no knowledge of English and U.S. culture, read alouds become a door into their new world, allowing them to bring across the threshold all of their current background knowledge about how language and literacy work. In fact, read alouds address the national professional standards for literacy because they provide the opportunity for children to be involved in reading a variety of genres for a variety of purposes.

We begin this chapter by explaining why and how language can be developed through interactive read alouds (Krashen, 2004). Then we present ideas for both primary and intermediate teachers regarding when and how to do read alouds in the classroom. In addition, we explain the use of language cognates to support instruction and considerations when choosing which books to use for read alouds. Finally, we discuss the assessment of students during read alouds, using the language arts standards as a guide. The lessons in this chapter are for use with ELL students with or without native language instruction, but we also present some additional information for classrooms that are providing native language instruction.

> **WHAT WE KNOW**
>
> Standard One of the National Council of Teachers of English/International Reading Association (NCTE/IRA, 1996) Standards for the English Language Arts states:
>
> "Students read a wide range of print and non-print texts to build an understanding of texts, of themselves, and of the cultures of the United States and the world; to acquire new information; to respond to the needs and demands of society and the workplace; and for personal fulfillment. Among these texts are fiction and nonfiction, classic and contemporary works."
>
> "Children read a wide range of literature from many periods in many genres to build an understanding of the many dimensions (e.g., philosophical, ethical, aesthetic) of human experience."

PURPOSE FOR READ ALOUDS

"Language is a socially shared code that uses a conventional system of arbitrary symbols to represent ideas about the world that are meaningful to others who know the same code" (Nelson, 1998, p. 26). In other words, language is shared socially; it is used by the members of a community. Many languages, including English, have a written code or arbitrary symbols that help the members of the community understand one another in a systematic way. The set of symbols carry meaning that, when combined, creates words and represents our feelings, our knowledge of the world, or whatever we intend to communicate to other members of the community. When we look at language development for ELL students, we need to take into consideration how the new language is presented, both verbally and in writing, and how the children are acquiring the English language code.

Vygotsky's (1986) theory of language acquisition helps us understand that children's comprehension and speech develop at different rates; our thought reaches more sophisticated levels sooner than our speech. In other words, teachers can read books to ELL students that are above their speaking level and provide opportunities for comprehending the new language aurally *and* improving their oral language abilities. Given this, we can understand how during read aloud, ELL students are able to comprehend some of the language they hear even though their speech level is limited.

> ### WHAT WE KNOW
>
> Vygotsky (1986) wrote that thought and speech have different roots in human-kind, thought being nonverbal and speech being nonintellectual in an early stage. But their development lines are not parallel—they cross again and again. At a certain moment around the age of 2, the curves of development of thought and speech, until then separate, meet and join to initiate a new form of behavior. That is when "thought becomes verbal and speech becomes rational" (Jiménez, 2004, p. 66). A child first seems to use language for superficial social interaction, but at some point this language goes underground to become the structure of the child's thinking. Krashen's (1981) *acquisition-learning hypothesis* seems to have been influenced by Vygotsky. Although Vygotsky speaks of *internalization of language*, while Krashen uses the term *language acquisition*, both are based on a common assumption: Interaction with other people is essential as children learn language (Schutz, 2004).

If teachers scaffold language through asking questions, talking about the story, and comparing and contrasting books and genres, children will improve their proficiency in using language that is just beyond their independent speaking abilities. If teachers make the experience very interactive and pause during the story with a specific purpose, children will come to comprehend a variety of structures in English: idioms, colloquial expressions, unusual vocabulary, idiomatic expressions, and cognates with their native language. Students will also recognize the similarities and differences between their native language and English.

Language development for ELL students requires more than just learning new words and their definitions; it requires the interaction and application of contextualized and decontextualized language structures (syntax), semantics, and the phonics of English. ELL students need to understand the relationship between these language systems and actual verbal communication in order to acquire and produce their new language (Freeman & Freeman, 2004).

We understand that in many classrooms teachers might have students at different language levels or reading levels, and in Chapter 2 we encouraged teachers to group students according to language proficiencies. If our suggestions do not meet the needs of your situation, we propose giving your ELL students a specific time to have read alouds just for them. This will help you address their needs and challenge them, and at the same time your English-speaking students will not dominate the conversation or become uninterested in the activity.

READ ALOUDS FOR K–2 ELL STUDENTS

Many of us remember how our family members read to us or told us stories when we were little. Some of those stories we can't forget, and they have a very special place in our hearts. Those wonderful characters, the incredible settings and problems, the words that the characters used, will be with us forever. When we hear the words, "big bad wolf," we immediately think of, "and he huffed and he puffed, and he blew the house down." Or perhaps, "'What big eyes you have, grandmother,' said little Red Riding Hood." Read alouds and oral stories have a special magic in children's lives. They transform children's experiences so much that sometimes the children believe they are part of the story; they identify completely with the character or the character's problems and adventures. Because of their power and magic, read alouds play a crucial role in children's literacy development in school.

Build on Before Reading: Purpose and Previewing. The first question we need to ask ourselves is, "What is the teaching purpose for this interactive read aloud?" Besides the most common purpose, comprehension (Harvey & Goudvis, 2000), we need to pay attention to two other important goals for ELL students: language development (semantics, syntax, and expression) and *building on* and providing background knowledge. Interactive read alouds provide structured opportunities for teaching language, teaching about language, and using students' background experiences to extend their knowledge to new concepts and ideas.

Having identified the purpose, teachers should take the time to preview the text with the children and set the goal for the reading. Taking the time to preview the book will result in better understanding going into the reading. Prompt the students to help them access information for use with the text.

- What does the illustration on the cover represent?
- How does the illustration and/or title relate to their lives?
- Why did the author choose that title?

Provide an overview of the story through a picture walk, a graphic organizer, or use of familiar text structure prompts. Previewing the title and the story, using objects, realia, and illustrations, will help students access their background knowledge about the topic and become primed for the vocabulary that is part of the text.

Explain During Reading: Focus on Strategies for Language Development and Comprehension. When working with ELL students, reading a book all the way through, with few stops for discussion, may result in students being captivated by the teacher's voice and the illustrations but little comprehension of the story being told. For ELL students, teachers need to stop frequently to ask questions, draw their attention to the meaning of the story up to that point, and help them interact with one another. The questions and prompts provide opportunities to explain specifics about how language is used, as well as discussing what the story is about.

As teachers read aloud to children, they are modeling the flow and fluency of written language and at the same time exposing the children to language structures that are specific to written language. Teachers can point out to children and talk about the way they are reading the text and why. For instance, in the traditional three pigs stories, the teacher reads, "And he huffed, and he puffed, and he *blew* the house down!" using a particular cadence and expression that she hopes will give the listener a sense of the wolf's malicious physical presence and intent. In *The True Story of the 3 Little Pigs* (Scieszka, 1996), the wolf whines, "Well I huffed, and I snuffed, and I sneezed a great sneeze," downplaying his carnivorous intentions and trying to play on the audience's sympathies for his cold. How the teacher reads these passages out loud can help ELL students understand how the written language and our use of voice work to provide information about the story beyond the words themselves. But teachers must make this transparent for children by talking explicitly about how they are reading and why.

Involve Students After Reading: Extending Comprehension. At the end, students may say they liked the story and even be able to bring up one or two points that they remember. You can check their understanding by asking them to talk to one another about the book (in their native language, if that is possible or necessary), draw pictures about their favorite part, or in the case of 2nd graders, complete sentence starters such as:

- I like the book because . . .
- The first thing that happened in the story was . . .
- The character got in trouble because . . .

If you give them sentence starters, make sure you discuss several possible answers they can choose from. This will help them connect reading, writing, and oral language development. We need to dig deep to make sure our students "get" what is going on in the text; this takes time, scaffolding, and many, many questions to help them.

READ ALOUDS FOR GRADES 3–5 ELL STUDENTS

Read alouds with older students provide supportive opportunities to engage them in both oral and written English that is more challenging than what they are able to do independently. There are three key components to read alouds for the upper grades that will help ELL students move their English comprehension and performance to a higher level.

1. Activating background knowledge. Older students have a wealth of knowledge about the world and how language works. Teachers need to use this knowledge to take students to the next level of understanding.
2. Stimulating high-level thinking and high-level language that is above their oral language proficiency. Using age-appropriate, high-level texts that are of interest to students will keep them engaged and push their language use to new levels. Ask high-level questions to facilitate critical thinking.
3. Engaging in talk to foster semantic and syntax development in English. Getting ELL students to talk about the story and the language used in the story will provide the support they need to articulate complex ideas.

Build on Before Reading: Background Knowledge. As we have explained, activating prior knowledge is one of the key components for students' learning. Studies refer to this strategy in literacy as one of the most important for students to use in understanding what they read and write (Escamilla, 1993; Keene & Zimmermann, 2007). During read alouds teachers often read books that require understanding the mainstream culture of the school and the community, and consequently children new to U.S. culture find them difficult to comprehend. In order for students to understand them, the stories need to be chosen carefully, *building on* what students already know in order to give them new language for talking about familiar topics. The purpose is not to provide just what they know; the purpose is to give the children the opportunity to apply their linguistic and content knowledge toward acquisition of the new language and of new concepts, both cultural and academic.

The read alouds provide a wonderful opportunity not only to build background knowledge but also to give the children the possibility of sharing their diverse understandings of the story. Through becoming familiar with certain meanings and concepts, and through discussing their ideas, children will be able to apply their knowledge to understanding the story and draw conclusions about the new world they are living in, such as that folktales are a part of the social and academic culture, diversity of opinion is valued, and various versions of a similar story are common.

For a read aloud, let's take the book *Cock-A-Doodle-Doo!* by Janet Stevens and Susan Stevens Crummel (1999). This book is based on the traditional folktale *The Little Red Hen.* At first look, teachers might think the story would be easy for intermediate students to understand and make connections to. Yet, for ELL students it could be difficult because they might never have read *The Little Red Hen.* Also, the humor that is in the book requires background knowledge and understanding of words with multiple meanings. The children will have to understand not only the vocabulary but the basic concept of the story in English; thus, it is important to build background knowledge before reading. Going over the pictures and using realia will make the story more comprehensible to the children.

Explain During Reading: Focus on Strategies for Language Development and Comprehension. In reading *Cock-A-Doodle-Doo!* realia is an essential teaching tool. The illustrations in the book will help, but photographs or, even better, samples of real flour, butter, and cakes will help even more. Also, since bringing live animals into the classroom is probably not a good idea (at least not for this story), plastic models of the animals will help children make the connections. (Note: Although stuffed toy pigs sometimes may look like real pigs, stuffed toy roosters usually don't look like real ones; therefore, stuffed toys don't make the best realia for this ESL instruction.)

Take advantage of read aloud time to address another of the important components for ensuring language development: stimulating high-level thinking and language above and beyond students' oral language proficiency. Active participation through questioning and discussion is essential for comprehension. Teachers cannot assume that students understand what is going on in the story just because they look attentive. A good reader will captivate children, even if they don't really understand what the reader is saying. But in the case of read alouds for ELL students, teachers need to make sure that the children *do* understand who the characters are, what the story is about, how the problem is resolved, and why everyone is happy (or sad, or confused) at the end. It is important to ask questions both during and after reading that focus on elements of the story, while getting the students involved in talking about their ideas related to the story. For example, during the story teachers can ask:

1. What has happened so far in the story?
2. Where does rooster get all the ingredients for the cake?
3. When will pig get to taste the cake?
4. Where are the dog, the cat, and the goose when rooster is cooking?

After having read through the story, teachers can ask:

1. Why did the rooster remember his great-grandmother's story?
2. Why were pig, turtle, and iguana confused about what to do?
3. How do you think rooster felt when the animals tried to help him?
4. How would you get your friends to help you cook?

The questions "what," "when," and "where" will help students to recall the story during the reading so they don't get lost. The questions "why" and "how" will help students reflect on their own understanding and will increase their level of conversation. As a result of the combination of the two levels of questioning, students will develop the contextualized language, or pure facts, and the

---

WHAT WE KNOW

Questions are an effective way to help students get into and think about text at literal and deep levels (Keene & Zimmermann, 2007; Raphael, 1986; Raphael, Highfield, & Au, 2006). Through predictions at the beginning, middle, and end of the story, students can use relevant information to speculate and infer what might happen (Keene & Zimmermann, 1986). The four levels of questions that Raphael (1986; Raphael, Highfield, & Au, 2006) calls Question Answer Relationship (QAR) can help teachers construct questions that monitor literal understanding and support students' critical thinking at more abstract levels. These four levels of questions are:

1. Right there—the information is easy to find in the text
2. Think and search—the information is in more than one place in the book
3. Author and you—some information is in the book, but the reader needs to use background knowledge as well
4. On my own—the answers come from the readers' background knowledge and personal opinions

---

decontextualized language that requires feelings, opinions, and higher levels of thinking.

Another of the key components in read alouds for older students is the use of student talk to foster the appropriate use of syntax and semantics in English. Teachers need to make sure they don't dominate the conversation, talking so much that the children don't get a chance to verbalize their ideas. It is important to give ELL students sufficient wait time; teachers can model this by being explicit and transparent about taking wait time for themselves and reminding students about taking wait time for themselves and one another. Talk about the fact that everyone needs "thinking time" (Walsh & Sattes, 2004). Remember that students in the first stages of learning the language must first translate the question, next compose the answer in their native language in their heads, and finally translate the answer to English before responding.

One common situation happens when teachers see that ELL children are "struggling" to put their ideas into words and may have trouble saying in English what they are thinking. Teachers, not wanting children to suffer or to feel inadequate because they are having difficulties, often will finish thoughts for the students or move on quickly, not giving enough think time for them to put their thoughts together. Another common occurrence is when teachers, with the best of intentions, want to avoid these problems altogether. In that case, they may just read through the book without stopping to talk about the story or without letting the children talk about the story.

We suggest using the *think, pair, share* activity in which everyone has think time, everyone gets a chance to rehearse their verbal response with a partner, and then some children get to share their responses with the whole group. This adds time to the interactive read aloud activity, certainly, but we have to remember that read aloud for ELL students is more than just exposing them to good books and language. We need to use this opportunity to actually build language, get them using vocabulary and English structures, and build background knowledge, all of which will increase their abilities to comprehend and use English.

Involve Students After Reading: Extending Comprehension. The main focus of read aloud is for the students to understand the story and increase their language proficiency. Language comprehension should be achieved not by the teacher or other students translating words into the native language, but through talk in English. Teachers can model and then encourage students to explain words and ideas using different English language that may be more comprehensible, along with physical acting out and the use of realia. Using one or two other English terms and lots of active involvement will help children understand the language in the story in a way that will allow them to remember and use it later.

After the read aloud, you may re-read the story the next day, helping the students to better understand the vocabulary and interact in other ways that require language and higher order thinking. There are several activities students can do after reading the book *Cock-A-Doodle-Doo!* that will help them further understand the story and apply their new language.

- Adapt the recipe using ingredients from their native lands
- Make a strawberry shortcake with the class, having some students go through the book and give instructions while the others do the cooking

- Role play the story
- Do a reader's theatre of the story
- Find other illustrated books about cooking and do compare and contrast activities with the vocabulary, characters, settings, conflict/resolution, and so forth (see Figure 3.1 for a selection of titles)

CONSIDERATIONS FOR STUDENTS WITH NATIVE LANGUAGE INSTRUCTION

When ELL students are receiving native language instruction, read alouds can be done in both languages to help students develop their understanding of written language, their understanding and production of oral language, and their understanding of academic concepts in both languages. In Chapter 2 we suggest that the schedule for kindergarten and 1st grade classrooms with native language should have a significant amount of time for read alouds in *both* native languages and English. For the rest of the grade levels, time spent depends on the expectations of the districts. Some districts stop native language instruction in the primary grades, some in the

---

FIGURE 3.1. Food Lovers' Illustrated Books

There are dozens of books about food and their ingredients that can be used with ELL students. These books are a natural way to access students' background knowledge and support their developing use of language and academic concepts. Here are a few of our favorite titles:

- *The Apple Cake* by Nienke van Hichtum
- *Hey, Pancakes!* by Tamson Weston, illustrated by Stephen Gammell
- *Malke's Secret Recipe* by David Adler, illustrated by Joan Halpern
- *Pancakes for Breakfast* by Tomie dePaola
- *Pancakes, Pancakes* by Eric Carle
- *Saturday Sancocho* by Leyla Torres
- *Stone Soup* by Marcia Brown
- *Thundercake* by Patricia Polacco
- *Wolf's Chicken Stew* by Keiko Kasza

The following website from the Pennsylvania Department of Education can be used to find additional titles: http://www.pafamilyliteracy.org/pafamilyliteracy/cwp/view.asp?a=224&Q=91717

---

intermediate. No matter when the children stop receiving formal native language instruction, if the teacher is bilingual, it would be helpful to allow time during the week for some read alouds in their native language. Time devoted to read alouds in both languages will help the students develop both languages and transfer skills and language from one to the other, especially when teachers focus on higher order thinking such as inferring and drawing conclusions (Cappellini, 2005).

LANGUAGE COGNATES: TRUE AND FALSE

Cognates can play important roles in students' English language development, especially if children are receiving native instruction. Interactive read alouds in English can be the connection between what ELL students know about language and what they are learning. Since many languages have a rich number of cognates with English, teachers need to constantly ask students about the similarities of words to their native language. In this way, students enhance their vocabulary by building on what they already know. In working with students who speak nonalphabetic languages, the use of cognates during instruction will happen more in oral language development than with written language. There are various resources teachers can use to find cognates. Here are two Web sites that are helpful.

http://www.latinamericalinks.com/spanish_cognates.htm
http://www.macmillandictionary.com/MED-Magazine/
    july2004/21-FalseFriends-Russian.htm

When teaching cognates it is important for teachers to know the definitions before using the words. Although cognates can support instruction because of pronunciation and spelling similarities, they might create confusion because the meaning and use of the words are not always the same across languages and cultures. It is important to check the meaning of the word and how it is used in the context of the text. Some of the resources available to teachers list only the words, without the definitions; this can lead to misunderstandings since words that look similar may have very different meanings. Figures 3.2 and 3.3 show examples of true and false cognates between Spanish and English.

Figure 3.2. Examples of True and Close Spanish/English Cognates

- *Autor–Author:* This one is easy. Both words mean the composer of a book, article, or other piece of writing.
- *Billón–Billion*: 1,000,000,000,000. This is the same in traditional British English but it is a trillion in American English. In other words, *billón* is a cognate in London but a false cognate in New York.
- *Principal–Principal:* The words share one meaning, the most important thing. However, in English it also means a school's director, while in Spanish you would call that person *el director*.

Figure 3.3. Examples of False Spanish/English Cognates

- *Bien Educado–Well Educated:* In Spanish, this means well behaved. In English, it means somebody who has acquired an academic education. This difference causes much confusion when teachers and parents are trying to communicate.
- *Envolver–Involve: Envolver* in Spanish is to wrap something up. When you want to convey the meaning of *involve*, use *participar* or *involucrar*.
- *Atender–Attend*: The Spanish means *to serve* or *to take care of, to attend to*. If you're talking about attending a meeting or a class, use *asistir*.
- *Complexión–complexion*: In Spanish, this refers not to one's skin, but to one's physiological build (a well-built man is *un hombre de complexión fuerte*). To speak of skin complexion, use *tez* or *cutis*.

CHOOSING TEXTS FOR READ ALOUDS

The choice of books for read alouds is an important consideration since these books might be used over 2 or more days, depending on the teacher's purpose and students' background knowledge. It is important to remember that ELL students are working to comprehend the story *and* developing language at the same time; therefore, it is helpful to read and re-read the story as many times as necessary.

When we choose books for read alouds, it is better to choose picture books, both fiction and nonfiction, rather than chapter books, even for older students. The illustrations support their understanding and grab their interest, and at the same time quality picture books have high-level vocabulary and interesting topics for all ages. There are excellent picture books for older students that will not make them feel they are using "baby" books. Along with interesting stories, some wonderful poems have been made into picture books for the upper elementary age group. There is also a wealth of high-quality nonfiction for older readers that has gripping photographs; these can be used for high-interest read alouds as well.

It is important to keep read aloud books at a high enough level so that students are exposed to more sophisticated language than they use during normal conversation. The topics and a certain amount of vocabulary should be familiar, but the book's language also should enrich and increase the students' bank of vocabulary and expressions. As we pointed out previously, their level of English does not necessarily match their higher level of cognitive understanding. Books at a 1st-grade level will not be appropriate for 5th-grade students, no matter how limited their English language is. Children who are read to on a regular basis begin to incorporate the language of the read aloud books into their own verbal and written language (Nathenson-Mejía, 1989). We want ELL students to learn to comprehend and use high-level, complex, sophisticated language, not get stuck at the "beginner's level" just because they are second language learners. For a selection of some of our favorite titles for older students, see Figure 3.4.

FIGURE 3.4. Picture Books for Grades 3–5

Here are several books that will appeal to older students. These books have themes, such as grandparents, relationships, and moving, that will build on and extend students' background knowledge.

Song and Dance Man by Karen Ackerman, illustrated by Stephen Gammell
Everybody Needs a Rock by Byrd Baylor, illustrated by Peter Parnall
The Gift of the Sacred Dog by Paul Goble
The Quilt Story by Tony Johnston, illustrated by Tomie dePaola
Love as Strong as Ginger by Lenore Look, illustrated by Stephen T. Johnson
Sister Anne's Hands by Marybeth Lorbiecki, illustrated by K. Wendy Popp
Almost to Freedom by Vaunda Micheaux Nelson, illustrated by Colin Bootman
Sitti's Secrets by Naomi Shihab Nye, illustrated by Nancy Carpenter
Mrs. Katz and Tush by Patricia Polacco
Grandfather's Journey by Alan Say
A Chair for my Mother by Vera B. Williams

ASSESSING INTERACTIVE READ ALOUDS

Interactive read alouds should be assessed with the main purpose of looking at language development and demonstrations of comprehension. On assessments based on the national and state standards for reading (NCTE/IRA, 1996), children are given standardized tests with multiple-choice questions about story elements, comprehension strategies, and higher order thinking. They are further expected to demonstrate their proficiencies by composing their ideas in constructed responses. Interactive read alouds will give the children exposure and practice in all of those elements and thus support their success on the standardized tests. While doing interactive read alouds, we suggest assessing children on some of the elements required by the standards. The checklist in Table 3.1 is an example and a suggestion of what teachers could do in their classrooms to assess children.

SUMMARY

Interactive read alouds for ELL students are an essential part of their literacy. If teachers develop language, focus on comprehension, *build on* and provide background knowledge, children will develop a strong base on which to comprehend independently and talk about the books they read during independent reading. In the following chapter we will look at the connection between read aloud and shared reading and how teachers can build on what they have taught during read aloud through shared readings.

Using voice expression, gestures, and even photos or realia to help ELL students comprehend is important; they need all the cues and clues they can get. Providing all of this support ensures that students acquire the vocabulary and language structures they need, and reinforces and expands on the concepts for their success in U.S. classrooms. If children don't have the opportunities to interact with read aloud stories, the language will be heard once, and then they will forget it. Language is something that we need to practice, over and over, and if children don't practice, it will be hard for them to acquire English. To be effective, read alouds for ELL students need to be structured with this specific focus (see Figure 3.5).

TABLE 3.1. Assessing Students During Interactive Read Alouds

Behaviors	No Evidence	Sometimes	Often
Engages during read aloud			
Speaks in complete sentences			
Approximates Standard English			
Answers are accurate from the text			
If applicable, uses two languages accurately			
Summarizes/retells the story in sequence and accurately			
Enjoys read alouds			
Uses comprehension strategies to understand the text			
Sustains meaning during the mini-lesson			
Demonstrates experience with a topic from the text			
Talks about the topic with expression and self-assurance			
Gives examples from the lesson			
Makes connections with the text			
Predicts based on past experiences			
Compares and contrasts own experiences with the text			

FIGURE 3.5. Reminders for Read Alouds with ELL Students

1. Choose age-appropriate books on familiar topics.
2. Develop a specific plan for the lesson.
3. Preview the book thoroughly and stop often to ask questions.
4. Use the book over at least 2 or more days to focus on strategies that build on one another.
5. Compare/contrast books, and have conversations about them.
6. Have students read, talk, draw, act out, and write about the book.
7. Help students develop language (listening, speaking, reading, and writing) through use and attention to language structures, semantics, syntax, and contextualized and decontextualized language.
8. Read a book at the students' cognitive level (1st-grade books are not usually appropriate for 4th-grade students).
9. For children who have native language instruction, read the book in both languages.

Teachers additionally can support ELL students' language acquisition by making language-to-language connections using cognates, talking about both the cognates that conserve meaning across languages and those where the meaning changes. Choosing age-appropriate texts for read alouds, both fiction and nonfiction, at levels just a bit higher than students' oral proficiency will keep their interest high and help to continually raise the level of their English language abilities.

Continuous assessment of ELL students' comprehension, engagement, and use of strategies during read alouds will help teachers identify the strengths to *build on* and the needs to address during shared and guided reading.

CHAPTER 4

Shared Reading: Learning Through Language

WHEN YOU ARE AT A football game or an event where the whole crowd is singing the national anthem, is that experience so powerful that you really believe you sing just like the featured vocalist? This experience is very similar to the power that shared reading produces for young readers (Peregoy & Boyle, 2005). When readers engage during shared reading, the teacher acts as the lead vocalist singing the national anthem, and the children are the crowd. They have strong guidance and support that help them feel that they "sing" just like the teacher.

When we talk about shared reading for ELL students, this power is also evident. The difference is that it needs to be more explicit, more stretched out, and, like the read alouds, shared reading needs to have a very specific reading instruction purpose that includes language development. Since the children are looking directly at the text, the language development is contextualized and children have the opportunity to learn reading strategies and verbalize their ideas. Shared reading is the perfect time for them to interact with the language socially and academically.

Shared reading builds on what students have learned in read aloud. But in shared reading, ELL students become involved in the act of reading itself, joining with the teacher to read from the shared text. This chapter will explain the purpose for shared reading, how to teach the language in context, and how to develop language for ELL students. We also will discuss choosing appropriate texts to use during shared reading and what to consider when assessing shared reading.

WHAT WE KNOW

In 1979, Don Holdaway began promoting structured shared reading as a way to recreate the wonderful relationship and teaching that parents and young children experience during lap readings. CREDE (2002) refers to these experiences as Instructional Conversations (IC), and explains, "IC achieves individualization of instruction; is best practiced during joint productive activity; is an ideal setting for language development; and allows sensitive contextualization, and precise, stimulating cognitive challenge" (teaching through conversation, par. 1).

PURPOSE FOR SHARED READING

From the foundational work of Holdaway in 1979 through the "Five Standards for Effective Pedagogy" of CREDE (2002), research has shown that the engaging techniques used in shared reading are effective for all learners. Shared reading helps all learners develop oral and written language proficiency. The purpose of shared reading is to learn language through language. When the students are exposed to a text during shared reading, they also are exposed to the five reading components—vocabulary, phonics, phonemic awareness, fluency, and most important, comprehension (National Reading Panel, 2000).

An overriding focus during shared reading, along with and based in students' comprehension, should be the opportunities children have to read, interact with, talk about, discuss, and explore the text. As Gibbons (2002) reminds us when she talks about the experience people have when they learn a second language, the hardest part is to express what we want to say. If teachers give children the opportunity to talk in the safe environment of shared reading, they are able to not only practice but also enhance their language abilities. The children need to continually build on previous instruction of English language, both contextualized and decontextualized; grammar structures; semantics; comprehension strategies; and pronunciation (Cappellini, 2005; Chen & Mora-Flores, 2006; Uribe, 2004).

During shared reading children can make connections visually between the known and the unknown in ways that will increase their comfort with the new language. These connections may be as simple as recognizing a familiar word in print or identifying with a familiar topic. For example, if a Spanish-speaking child hears and sees the word "favorite," he or she can make the connection with the word *favorito*. If the text focuses on a familiar topic, such as food, animals, or homes, the children will make connections with concepts they already know and experiences they already have had, making these topics more comprehensible (Echevarria et al., 2004; Gibbons, 1991; Krashen, 1981). These connections will support understanding and help students to feel successful. A feeling of success will lead to further learning.

Shared reading is a wondrous experience in which the teacher and the children work together to acquire new proficiencies and concepts by using the children's zone of proximal development (Vygotsky, 1986). During shared reading the teacher's lead enables the students to read out loud words and phrases that they sometimes are unable to read or understand independently. This supported oral reading helps ELL students develop fluency in reading English. Teachers have the opportunity to *build on* their modeling of oral reading from read aloud, to *explain* how and why English is read in particular ways, and to *involve* students in supported oral reading as they all read together.

Since everyone reads the text out loud together while focusing on the teacher's lead, shared reading is also the perfect time to lower what Krashen (1981) calls students' "affective filter," the barrier students put between themselves and learning when they are uncomfortable. The supportive nature of shared reading allows ELL students to feel successful and to interact more with the language.

Although ELL children may be socialized in English (able to get along with English-speaking peers, speak with teachers), they do not necessarily have adequate language to interact academically with content material. Shared reading gives teachers opportunities to scaffold academic language by connecting "school social language" to "school academic language." Developing academic language is important for understanding transitions in texts, such as "however," "in the meantime," and "moreover." It is also essential for understanding expository text structures, comprehending academic questions, and doing academic writing. However, ELL students also require a third level of language, social academic language, to understand and express the high level of language in literacy communities. Social academic language is necessary to collectively cooperate in book talks and work together on literacy and content projects (Dutro & Moran, 2003; Gottlieb, 2006).

WHAT WE KNOW

Cummins (1981) explains that ELL students learn social language, or BICS (basic interpersonal communicative skills), in a different way and on a different time-table from academic language, or CALP (cognitive academic language proficiency). Dutro and Moran (2003) build on this concept, giving specific techniques for addressing these distinctions in order to ensure that students get the specific academic language that they need to be successful.

SHARED READING FOR K–2 ELL STUDENTS

When the basis of our lessons for ELL students in shared reading is language comprehension, reading the story comes more naturally, since the children will be working with the teacher to understand what they are learning to read. A focus on language comprehension also will help them see the purpose of specific aspects of written language. Language structures make sense within a particular, meaningful context, and when readers comprehend the language and the story, the particular language structures being used make more sense (see Figure 4.1). It is a symbiotic relationship: When they understand the language they can understand the story, and when they understand the story they can understand the style of language.

FIGURE 4.1. Language Specific to Genre

In some of the traditional story versions of *The Three Little Pigs,* the first line reads, "Once upon a time there were three little pigs who went out into the world to seek their fortunes." Leaving home to seek one's fortune is a common theme in European-based folktales. We want ELL students to understand this concept and to have access to the language they will find in many folktales. Teachers may be tempted to use simpler language in an effort to make comprehension easier. However, if teachers can help students understand the phrase, "went out into the world to seek their fortunes," they will have helped the students enrich their language, *and* will have laid a foundation for comprehension and connections with other books.

In *The Three Little Javelinas,* a western version of the little pigs folktale, author Susan Lowell uses the phrase, "trotted away to seek their fortunes." If they have already spent time learning what the phrase means in the traditional version, ELL students will have an advantage when they are exposed to this variation or other folktales that use this phrase.

In order to make the shared reading more successful for ELL students, teachers need to plan the instruction for the lesson purposefully and focus on particular aspects of the language, especially grammar. During shared reading for native English-speaking children, we don't have to worry too much about the way they will put words together in a sentence. They bring to school an internalized language grammar, since the structure of one's native language is formed during our first years of life (Guasti, 2004). For example, when talking about a girl, a young native English-speaking child will always say "she." ELL students, on the other hand, need to learn when to use "she" or "he," "hers" or "his," and even after learning the rule, non-native speakers may have to think about this pronoun usage for years before being able to produce it automatically.

When teachers plan shared reading for young ELL children, we suggest using a text over a few days, choosing a different language aspect to work on each day or two. The ideas that follow are essential instructional points for young children; however, the specific instructional targets depend on the needs of the students. These strategies are not meant to be used in a certain order, and they also might be useful for teaching intermediate ELL students.

Focusing on High-Frequency Words

For ELL students these words tend to be function words, such as *a, the, and, that*; time or place words, *then, where, while*; verbs, *went, bring, write*; and pronouns *he, she, their*. These words need to be taught in context since their meaning is often very difficult to explain if taught in isolation. Also, children need to have practice in formulating sentences in which they can include those words, for example, the articles *a* and *an*. It is important that teachers present these words within a complete text and also provide different examples of their use. Here again we have a situation where native English speakers have little difficulty using *a* or *an* appropriately, but ELL students need explicit and repeated instruction in a meaningful context to be able to remember and use this grammar structure. We can't just ask, "Which sounds right?" because for an English language learner they both sound equally strange or equally correct. As you discuss the words found in the shared reading text, encourage and support students in formulating sentences that use these words.

Using Prepositions

Prepositions, such as *in, on, under, up, over, at,* and *through,* can be quite confusing for ELL students. Even though other languages have prepositions, their use may differ greatly. For example, in Spanish the word *en* is used for both "in" and "on"; therefore it is often very hard for Spanish-speaking children to know and remember when they need to use which of these two English prepositions. A variety of activities that get students involved in repetition and review will help, as well as physical "acting out" of prepositions and prepositional phrases. Teachers can engage students in games of hunting for prepositions in texts, then *explain* why the text uses a particular preposition in a particular phrase. Sentences can be lifted from familiar texts, and teachers can support students in generating various other sentences that follow the same patterns. As with most of the activities for shared reading, a strong connection to shared writing will help students to apply and internalize their learning.

Finding Word Patterns

The patterns teachers decide to work on, such as *aught, ack, ake, ight,* need to come from their students' mistakes. Often teachers spend a long time teaching patterns such as "cat, sat, mat"; however, if those patterns exist in the students' native language, teaching them should take much less time than teachers spend. More important, it is tempting for teachers to spend a long time on simple patterns that students will see and have opportunities to use frequently, and not progress to the more complex patterns that may prove challenging but are important for higher levels of proficiency. As children are learning about English graphophonetics, patterns such as "-at" and "ack" make sense to them; they have pretty straightforward sound/symbol correspondence. However, "-aught, -ought, -ight," and "-ould" are difficult to figure out and remember. Therefore, teachers need to collect information from the assessment of children's reading and writing to find out what patterns the children are able to read and write fairly consistently (not necessarily perfectly) and what patterns are giving them more trouble.

Practicing English Pronunciations

There will be great variation in students' abilities to acquire standard pronunciations. Typically, the younger the student, the more quickly and native-like his or her pronunciation will develop. However, how much opportunity children have had to use English also will make a difference. If 4- to 6-year-olds are in classrooms that do not encourage the use of English—in other words, if students are passive learners—then their pronunciation will develop more slowly. If teachers read stories *to* students and then *with* them, children will begin to acquire the correct pronunciations. Also, through repeated interactive engagement with the language, children's approximations continually will take on the more standard pronunciations. When we raise babies, we do not spend time making them repeat a word over and over until they pronounce the word correctly. We talk to them and we give them the opportunity to tell us their ideas with approximations of the language until they eventually, over time, pronounce the words accurately. That is what teachers need to do as ELL students are learning to pronounce English words. They should allow the students to have the time they need to learn to pronounce the words correctly, but at the same time give them many, many opportunities to hear standard pronunciation and practice it. This does not mean teachers shouldn't teach pronunciation—they should. However, endless drills will not help and may hinder students' willingness to try.

SHARED READING FOR GRADES 3–5 ELL STUDENTS

Shared reading for intermediate children is planned in much the same manner as for primary children. The biggest difference is that the text and the English structures are more sophisticated. The purpose is still to develop language and choose a different aspect of the language to work on each day or two if needed. It is important to pay close attention to a variety of features of the text that will be used and to offer the possibility of using the text more than once in order to work on different aspects of the language. When reading a book for the first time, teachers should focus on supporting comprehension of the text. The second time through they could help the children understand and use particular text structures, such as refrains, questions, or dialogue (these conversations are also useful for primary students but the language is less sophisticated). The third time through the teacher could help students find certain words, such as adjectives. The text could offer many ways to focus on small bits of language. The ideas that follow are essential instructional points for intermediate children.

Using Meaningful Affixes

An affix is a small piece of language, such as *-ed*, *-ing*, *pre-*, or *de-*, that has no meaning on its own, but can change the meaning of not only a word but an entire sentence. It is not enough to tell students that *-ed* means something done in the past and *-ing* means it's being done right now. These are abstract notions that language learners find difficult to remember and use without a great deal of contextual practice.

Look for a few familiar texts that have several common affixes. Use this set of texts to teach the affixes, focusing on one at a time in the beginning. For example, with early English learners you may spend a few days working on the suffix *-ing*. When you are ready to work on *-ed*, use the same text set so you are reviewing and reinforcing *-ing* as you are working on *-ed*. Every time you read these and other texts, remind the students of what they learned previously about those affixes you've already worked on. *Build on* what they know from their daily language use. Get students to talk about what they are doing now, using *-ing*, and what they did yesterday, using *–ed*. For prefixes, talk with students about how they "*pre*view," "*pre*dict," "*pre*write," and so forth.

Understanding Homophones

Homophones, such as *to, too, two*; *here, hear*; *there, their, they're*; *bare, bear*, take a great deal of work and patience to learn correctly because in addition to sounding the same, they are usually very similar in how they are spelled. ELL students must learn the various meanings of what to them is *one* word (to, too, and two = /too/; hear and here = /hir/). They must learn the varied but similar spellings, and then learn to use the context of the sentence or paragraph to help them decide which of those meanings to apply. For example, in the sentence, "Animals construct their own habitat," if children don't know what "habitat" or "construct" means, they will not understand the word "their" or its use. To see the word "their" does not immediately signal a possessive for an English Language Learner as it might for a native speaker. An ELL student might interpret this sentence to mean, "Animals make something over there."

We need to remember that it can take English Language Learners years to gain an automatic understanding and use of these words. Teachers can support them through instruction, review, resources, and lots of patience.

Recognizing Homographs

Homographs, such as *read*, *bow*, *tear*, *live*, and *lead*, pose the same problem. They need to be understood in a meaningful context in order to know what they mean and how to say them. There are two levels of proficiency working at the same time, comprehension and pronunciation. The important thing is that teachers spend time teaching the words within familiar and meaningful contexts. They should provide various opportunities to remind students what they've learned and to give the students time to apply their learning with different texts. When teachers see students problem solving the meaning and the pronunciations of these words as they read and write, the teachers will know they have acquired this particular concept of the English language.

Practicing English Pronunciation

For various reasons, students who are 10–15 years old and who are new to English may have more difficulty with pronunciation than younger students. The older students' muscles used in producing speech are not accustomed to producing English sounds, their ears are not accustomed to hearing the sounds, and they may be more reluctant than young children to practice in public. However, here again it is important to provide many and varied opportunities for them to hear the standard models of English and then to use the language themselves. No matter how old we are, the more we practice a new language, the better we will get at using it.

One more factor to recognize is how much time English learners spend with native English speakers. If students are spending all of their playground and class time with students who speak their native language, they will use English less often and their pronunciation will develop more slowly. Teachers should *never* forbid students to use their native language. However, they should create many opportunities for students to work and play in mixed-language groups.

Learning More Complex Grammar Structures

Grammar structures, such as the placement of adjectives and adverbs, how we signify tense, and where we place pronouns and articles, require explicit instruction. However, they will be integrated into students' English language schemata only if students are provided opportunities to put them into practice. Children need to *use* the language, while at the same time learning the grammar; both components go together. Let's go back to the example of the way babies acquire language. They don't learn the grammar and then begin to talk, nor do they learn to speak and then learn the grammar. Actually they do both at the same time, transferring their developing knowledge and abilities back and forth, building one upon the other.

SHARED READING FOR STUDENTS WITH NATIVE LANGUAGE INSTRUCTION

For ELL students receiving instruction in their native language, literacy foundations increase in English as teachers phase English into the literacy block and increase reading and writing activities in English. The transition happens gradually over years, and the language of instruction changes according to students' needs and abilities. The format for shared reading is basically the same regardless of whether students receive native language instruction. What changes is the language of instruction. It is important to use native language texts that *build on* students' background knowledge and follow up with English texts on the same topics, continually spiraling back to and building on what they know, in either language.

During shared reading the students and the teacher read texts together, and the books provide the opportunity for transfer of skills and language acquisition. The group interaction creates a supportive environment in which the students can build concepts about print and learn how to use strategies to become better readers using phonics, structure, and semantic clues. The main focus is always comprehension, but at the same time attention is paid to vocabulary, grammar, and idiomatic expressions. In addition, shared reading helps increase opportunities for those who receive native language instruction to transfer concepts, compare and contrast language sounds and print, and engage in the high-order thinking skills required to have a successful transition into academic English.

SAMPLE SHARED READING LESSON

The following lesson, taught by Maria, illustrates how a teacher can use shared reading to develop language with ELL students.

Grade Level: Third

Book: In My Momma's Kitchen by Jerdine Nolen, illustrated by Colin Bootman. (This book can be used with 4th and 5th graders as well.)

This lesson uses the first story in the book, "First in Line," and focuses on

1. Vocabulary comprehension, especially idiomatic expressions: *first in line, made-up, burst in, scholarship, I am pleased to inform you, hugged real tight*
2. High-frequency words: *everything, without*
3. Word endings: "-ight"
4. Prepositions: *over, around*

The lesson can be done over 5 days; each day focuses on one teaching point.

Day One: Build On

Introduce the story by presenting vocabulary that connects the story to previous instruction and helps the students become familiar with words and phrases they might not understand. Build on what they already know from school and home. Expand their understanding through explanation and teaching of particular idiomatic expressions.

> *T*: What do you think it means to be first in line at home?
> *Boy*: Is like you know, like everyday your parents arrive home and you are already there.
> *T*: You're first; you are the first person when you get home.
> *Girl*: Like you are the leader.

Day Two: Explain

Read the story with the children and then teach about specific vocabulary, cognates, and idioms that have similar meaning but can be a bit confusing if the students don't fully understand them. Read the story for the second time with the students. Then discuss various words and phrases.

> *T*: OK, now it says here, "I am pleased to inform . . ." What does that mean, *I am pleased to inform*?
> *Girl*: I want to tell you.
> *T*: Exactly, I want to tell you. Inform means that they are telling you. This is another language-to-language word. What is the word in Spanish?
> *Students*: *información, informar*.

Day Three: Involve

Before teaching the lesson, highlight the two high-frequency words in the text. Ask the students to give different examples of sentences with the words.

Create a list of the words in the story that have the "-ight" sound. Then ask the children to offer some other known words that have the same ending.

> *T*: Very good, if it's tight, how am I going to spell that?
> *Students*: T-I-G-H-T
> *Girl*: might   M-I-G-H-T
> *Girl*: right   R-I-G-H-T
> *T*: OK, give me a sentence with the word *light*.

> *Boy*: The sun gives us light.
> *T*: Now give me a sentence with the word *tight*.
> *Boy*: These shoes are tight.
> *Girl*: My grandma hugs me tight.

Day Four: Involve

With the students, create sentences with the high-frequency words. Ask the students to give examples of sentences with the word *everything*.

> *T*: So far you have given me a short sentence, but you haven't given me a long sentence.
> *Girl*: I like everything around the school.
> *Boy*: I went to the school and they had everything I needed.

Day Five: Involve

Have the students role play the prepositions *around* and *over*. Prepositions can give English Language Learners a great deal of trouble. This review with some physical activity helps students remember what the words mean. Once they have acted out the prepositions, ask them to use these words in sentences.

> *T*: Very good. Now what I would like you to do is to give me a sentence with *over*.
> *Girl*: My friend went over to the house.
> *Girl*: I went over the fence.

CHOOSING TEXTS FOR SHARED READING

Repetition and reinforcement of concepts is essential. When teachers choose texts for shared reading, they need to relate the reading with what they are working on elsewhere during the literacy block. Whatever large *new* idea a teacher is trying to teach, whether it is a new concept, such as gardening, or a new text structure, such as personal narrative, *that* is what should be reinforced across read aloud, shared reading, and even guided reading. For example, if you are reading personal narratives during read alouds, it helps if the shared reading material is a short story or big book that has the same text structure (personal narrative). That way the children can make connections not only with content but also with the language structure. Children acquire language when they are able to transfer and use it over and over. It is fine to use the same book in both read aloud and shared reading, but it is not necessary. However, if different books are used, something about them should connect them to each other, the topic, and/or the structure to build from one to the other.

As explained in Chapter 2, shared reading texts need to be at the ELL students' cognitive levels. That is, teachers should use texts that are a bit above the students' independent proficiency. Shared reading is the bridge that can avoid keeping ELL children on a low reading level, especially if they are proficient readers in their native language. We cannot stress enough that, when children are readers in their native language, the texts used in English need to provide literacy connections to their academic lives and background knowledge, and need to be at their cognitive grade level. Working with grade-level materials will help students continue to move forward in their literacy acquisition and as an added benefit will help them perform on the state's standardized tests.

ASSESSING SHARED READING

When teachers assess shared reading for ELL students, they are assessing language proficiency simultaneously. They need to identify the areas of reading *and* language proficiency where a child needs help. Table 4.1 is a sample assessment checklist for ELL students that teachers can use during or after shared reading lessons.

SUMMARY

Teachers need to *build on* what students know while at the same time providing the new concepts and language that students need. Teachers need to *explain* and *involve* students so that the new strategy is made easy and repeated in different contexts. Teachers need to *build on, explain,* and *involve* students in small increments, baby steps, over an extended period of time. Strategies and language need to be introduced in a logical and systematic way. For example, focus on one general aspect of the language for a few days, provide

TABLE **4.1. Shared Reading Assessment Checklist**

Shared Reading Behaviors	No Evidence	Sometimes	Often
Engages during the reading of the text			
Uses verb tenses correctly in his/her sentences			
Uses context clues to recognize new vocabulary			
Uses picture clues to problem solve words			
Keeps track of the grammar taught in current and previous mini-lessons			
Keeps track of the phonics taught in the mini-lesson			
Keeps track of prepositions, homophones, and homographs in current and previous mini-lessons			
Reads with fluency and expression			

small amounts of information that build on one another every day, and engage students in active use and generation of the type of language being worked on. Shared readings will give teachers the opportunity to *build on* what the students already know and create a written record of what students have learned and are able to do. Both teachers and students can refer to this record of learning as they continue to teach and learn.

During shared reading teachers give the children the opportunity to learn, use, and create their own strategies for learning, understanding, and developing language. Read alouds and shared reading contain structures that help teachers to release more and more learning responsibility to the children, since they provide support for students to immediately use what they are learning. Teachers gradually can decrease the amount of support they provide so students gain independence and success in using the strategies ever more independently.

We should remember that English Language Learners need to learn effective reading strategies, but they also need to learn the subtleties of the English language and the characteristics of U.S.

culture. Read aloud and shared reading are wonderful opportunities for teachers to help students create bridges between the knowledge they have of their native language and culture and the new knowledge about English and U.S. culture. It is important to remember that all these components and structures of the language are best acquired within the meaningful context of familiar texts and topics, making choice of text an important component of planning. These different lessons do not have to be done on sequential days or even in the same week, but being able to return to a familiar book for several lessons will ensure that the instruction is embedded in meaningful context.

CHAPTER 5

Guided Reading: Learning About Language

G UIDED READING IS SMALL-GROUP instruction that builds on what students have learned from read aloud and shared reading. In guided reading teachers provide support as students become more independent, reading silently or out loud and applying what they know about semantics, syntax, and grapho-phonetics. Some methodologies call it needs-based instruction; others call it guided practice (Cappellini, 2005; Fountas & Pinnell, 2001; Taberski, 2000). Whatever the name, the goal is to instruct students with a text that they can read with an accuracy level of 90%, with teacher support, for decoding and comprehension.

When we talk about guided reading for students who are English Language Learners, we have similar concepts in mind. A small number of ELL students need to be grouped together to meet their specific reading needs. However, the grouping has specific goals because of the students' developing English language proficiency.

In this chapter we will discuss what teachers need to consider as they organize groupings for guided reading. We also will look at the goals for guided reading instruction based on the National Reading Panel (NRP, 2000) five components, plus other aspects of reading that are essential for English Language Learners. This chapter will provide information on choosing appropriate texts for ELL students and on how to assess ELL students' reading through conferences and what to look for.

GROUPING CONSIDERATIONS

When grouping ELL students for guided reading, a teacher needs to look at their reading backgrounds. They might be decoding the text with 90% accuracy, but their comprehension could be very limited due to their limited knowledge of the English language and culture. Usually children who have some literacy background in their native language are able to decode texts that sometimes they do not understand. For that reason, as we discussed in Chapter 2, we recommend grouping students according to age, English language levels, and/or the extent of literacy background knowledge in their native language. This grouping will help in determining the instructional needs they have and the language development the teachers need to address.

As we pointed out previously, 1st graders and 4th graders have *completely* different cognitive and psychological needs, and for that reason should not be grouped together for guided reading instruction. Some programs group English-speaking students by reading level, and older ELL students who are early English Language Learners often end up with 1st graders or in some cases even with kindergarten children. The fact that they lack English language does not mean that they should be placed at that level of reading instruction. How teachers scaffold language acquisition for a 9- or 10-year-old child should be *very* different from instruction for a 6- or 7-year-old. Teachers' attention to appropriate scaffolding will help older students read grade-level materials. If students are grouped by age, *and* by language abilities, then teachers can plan a guided reading lesson to address language development at an age-appropriate level.

SPECIFIC GOALS FOR INSTRUCTION: THE FIVE READING COMPONENTS PLUS

It is important to be specific about what we want the children to achieve during guided reading. Guided reading is the opportunity for children to have their needs addressed in both language and reading in a small-group setting. This allows the children to take risks and interact in a supportive environment because everyone in the group is at similar language levels. The children are doing most of the work, and the teacher is there to facilitate and develop language and reading skills (Diller, 2007). Although students in the group may not be at the exact same reading level, because they are at similar English language levels, they will have similar needs that can be addressed in the small-group setting.

WHAT WE KNOW

The National Reading Panel (2000) and the North West Regional Educational Laboratory (NWREL, 2007) have definitions and explanations of the five components of reading. Here is a brief explanation of each one adapted from the NWREL definitions.

1. Phonemic awareness is the knowledge that words are made of a combination of individual sounds and the ability to blend them into words.
2. Phonics is the relationship between language sounds and written letter(s). By connecting the sound and the written letter, children will be able to decode words in reading and put words into writing.
3. Fluency helps students read text accurately and smoothly at a pace that supports comprehension.
4. Vocabulary development expands students' knowledge of the language and the meaning of words.
5. Reading comprehension strategies help students engage in intentional thinking about what they read and to go deeper in their understanding of text.

The National Reading Panel (2000) reviewed research on five specific reading components that are important in helping students improve their ability to read. The components are phonemic awareness, phonics, fluency, vocabulary development, and comprehension. We agree that vocabulary, phonics, fluency, comprehension, and phonemic awareness are essential components for successful reading (Freeman & Freeman, 2004). However, when we talk about reading and writing for ELL students, we need to go beyond the five reading components, and we need to consider them in a different order. It is essential to look at specific aspects of language development, the order of development that makes sense for English Language Learners, and the implications these aspects and order have for each of the components.

Along with the five components, teachers need to think about how students are using the four cuing systems (Pearson, 1976; Routman, 1994). Proficient readers and writers use the four cueing systems to help them make sense of text: semantics, the meaning of language; syntax, the grammar structure; grapho-phonetics, the sound/symbol relationship; and pragmatics, the situation and purpose for language use. Teachers need to help ELL students pay attention to all of these components as they learn to read in English. The four cueing systems are embedded in the NRP's five components and our "plus" components. We will discuss the cueing systems further in Chapter 6.

In the discussion that follows we have put the NRP components in an order that we believe makes sense for English Language Learners' needs, except for comprehension. Comprehension needs to be considered first, last, and continuously throughout teaching. ELL students need to work on making meaning of what they are doing *all the time*. Every lesson taught on every component needs to be embedded in meaningful contexts. We will specifically discuss comprehension after the other NRP components, but its importance in all the areas cannot be overstated. At the end of the section we explain our "plus" components, necessary for the language and literacy of ELL students.

Vocabulary

Vocabulary development comes first because without knowledge of some words in English, ELL students will have no basis for understanding at all. Vocabulary enriches children's language and helps them to develop comprehension through concept development and word usage. However, vocabulary is under the big umbrella of oral language development—the interaction between social and academic language. The texts for elementary children often include and require the use of language that people use socially, but it is not exactly the everyday language children use outside of school. When we talk about vocabulary and oral language development, we do not mean only a list of words ELL students need to know. Rather, we mean the form, use, and semantics, all based in a meaningful context, of those words that help children to understand the texts.

As we have mentioned before, vocabulary needs to be developed based on background knowledge the students already have. For early learners of English, topics such as home, school, and food are important bridges into English. For intermediate and more proficient English learners, basing instruction in existing background knowledge is still important, but vocabulary development needs to take them further academically. When talking about homes, move into architectural styles, materials, location, building structures, construction processes, historical developments, neighborhood evolutions, and so forth. These topics are grounded in their own experiences but broaden their vocabulary, their understanding of the world, and their critical thinking. (See Figure 5.1 for further suggestions about developing vocabulary.)

FIGURE 5.1. Ideas for Teaching Vocabulary and Oral Language Development

- Plan specific questions about the text's vocabulary and content to focus on vocabulary development.
- Do illustration walks (pictures, photos, charts, graphs, maps) to talk about what students see, using vocabulary that will appear in the text. This is important for older students as well as younger children.
- Develop sentence structure knowledge and link vocabulary work to language structure: parts of speech, conjugating verbs, prefixes/suffixes, descriptive language placement, and so on. Use familiar texts, pulling out sentences from the text to focus on.
- Connect vocabulary instruction during read alouds, shared reading, and guided reading.
- Practice known words in different contexts and different times during the literacy block *and* content instruction (science, math, social studies, art, music, etc.).
- Model and talk about how students can express their ideas in English and how you decide to say something in a particular way. Make your thinking about how you use the language transparent.
- Access and build background knowledge, remembering that ELL students usually don't have the same concepts and perspectives for ideas we may consider common (see Chapter 1).
- Discuss the texts using the pictures/illustrations; make direct connections between the words and the illustrations.
- Encourage the children to talk to one another about the topic or concept.
- Focus the lesson on the new concept, using familiar language.
- Help students begin to articulate their thinking process as they discuss and read for understanding.
- Have students share some of their comments/personal information about the text. The more students talk and use the new vocabulary and structures, the more familiar they become.

Phonemic Awareness and Phonics

When teaching ELL students phonics, keep in mind that it is very difficult for them to distinguish isolated sounds in English due to their native language sounds. Children acquire language sounds and syntax between birth and 5 years old. Consequently, focusing on isolated sounds and assessing children on these isolated sounds will delay their progress in reading (Houk, 2005). ELL students acquire both phonemic awareness and phonics when teachers read *to* them, read *with* them, and encourage them to practice reading out loud.

It is tempting to spend a great deal of time on phonemic awareness and phonics with ELL students, since they need to learn the sound/symbol system of English, and they won't be able to read if they don't master decoding. However, "phonics first and foremost" is not an effective strategy. Teachers need to embed phonemic awareness instruction within meaningful oral language development activities such as songs, poems, word games, discussions, and role playing. Teachers need to embed phonics instruction within readings and discussions of whole, familiar texts and within writing instruction (see Figure 5.2 for further suggestions). It is essential to teach the parts of language within language as a whole. To *build on, explain,* and *involve* students in learning these components of the language, teachers should review, reinforce, and reteach when needed. Isolated skill lessons on blends, digraphs, and diphthongs will not help ELL students.

FIGURE 5.2. Ideas for Teaching Phonemic Awareness and Phonics

- Use daily life words and interesting sophisticated words (don't keep the students at the "easy" level too long).
- Work orally with fun and familiar songs, poems, and chants.
- Use these songs, poems, and chants in written form to focus on the sound/symbol system.
- Use a familiar book during guided reading to focus on the sound/symbol system.
- Decode by analogy with familiar words; use cognates to help students.
- Use pictures and other illustrations to support decoding.
- Connect to the sounds learned during shared reading.
- Connect to sounds that ELL students know from their first language.
- Read books at students' comprehension level, even if they are having trouble with decoding.

On the other hand, there are students who pick up decoding and pronunciation very quickly, but who do not capture the understanding of the words or language structures they need to comprehend what they are reading. These children need to be encouraged to stop frequently and talk about what is going on in the story. They need to learn to use text and illustration clues to help them create meaning. As we have said before, English Language Learners need everything all at once, and all the time!

Fluency

Fluency includes accuracy (reading the words with correct pronunciation), automaticity (reading high-frequency words or other known words without sounding them out), and the prosody of the language (reading with expression, looking at the punctuation and rhythm of the text). Therefore, it is a good idea to build fluency during shared reading and reinforce it during guided reading. As explained in Chapter 4, teacher support during oral/choral reading will help students read the words more accurately, and teacher-supported discussion will help them talk more deeply about the book. During guided reading the teacher reviews fluency strategies that were taught in shared reading and reinforces the ELL students' use of these strategies.

Comprehension

Comprehension is the most important of the five reading components. If students, whether native or non-native English speakers, do not comprehend what they are reading, then their reading experiences are empty, and they will have no motivation to continue. All students need to work on comprehension using texts that *build on* and extend their background knowledge. However, the texts used with ELL students will differ depending on the age and English proficiency of the students in the guided reading group.

With primary students who are monolingual non-English, we suggest having several texts that *build on* the same topic. For example, if they are reading about bears, they could have a text—very basic to begin with—that says, "The bear is brown. The bear is white. The bear is black." After working with this text, the teacher would continue with a text—again, basic, but with a definite increase in the reading level—that says, "The white bear is eating. The brown bear is drinking. The black bear is swimming." Next the teacher could use a text that says, "The white bear is eating fish. The brown bear is drinking water. The black bear is swimming in the river." The idea is to *build on* previous reading, vocabulary, and comprehension in small and meaningful increments. By continuing with the same topic but with increased vocabulary and syntax structures, the students not only understand, but also build comprehension and fluency in their reading (see Figure 5.3). Of course, as we've said many times already, much of the teaching and use of these texts should happen first in read aloud and shared reading to prepare students for the more focused small guided reading groups.

Often, young ELL students are given texts that go from topic to topic, but stay on the same reading level; thus it becomes very difficult for the children to advance to another level due to their language limitations. If teachers use books that carry forward the same topic and increase vocabulary, language structure, and concept complexity gradually, then students will improve and increase their reading abilities and their language development.

FIGURE 5.3. Ideas for Teaching Comprehension

- Focus on both literal and inferential comprehension; don't let students get stuck at a superficial level of understanding.
- Continually access and build background knowledge.
- Connect genre throughout reading and writing instruction.
- Connect to comprehension strategies taught during read aloud and shared reading (determine importance, infer, etc.).
- Stop often and make sure the children understand; get them to explain.
- Help the students generate questions about information in the reading.
- Teach students to put text information into graphic organizers: story element charts, storyboards, t-charts, compare and contrast, and so on.
- Prompt the students by asking:

    Can you tell me what happened in the story?
    Have you had a similar experience?
    What is the author trying to tell us?
    What does this word mean? Why is the author using this
        word if it means . . . ? (for multiple meanings)
    Can you tell me with your own words what is going on?
    What do you know about the topic?

With intermediate children, teachers can use a more sophisticated text that is already familiar to them and *build on* the concept of that text. Having a text set that focuses on a given topic will help develop and extend vocabulary. But with intermediate students the texts do not have to be quite as closely related to one another as do the texts for younger students. For example, a text set about bears could include an expository book on bears, a poem about bears, and a "Time for Kids" or "Ranger Rick" article on bears. Consequently, teachers need to plan their guided reading instruction and materials around both comprehension and language development.

The Plus Components

In addition to the five NRP components discussed above, teachers of ELL students need to pay attention to four more components in order to facilitate language and literacy development. First, primary and intermediate students need to have *both* vocabulary and high-frequency words (see Chapter 4). Second, teachers need to help ELL students learn and apply English language structures (grammar/syntax). Third, in order to comprehend text and become good readers, ELL students need to have background knowledge related to what they are reading (see Chapter 1). Finally, to optimize learning, teachers need to carefully select the texts they are using, taking all of the other "five components plus" into account.

Drawing on the work of Jan Richardson (2004), we have developed a chart with nine components of learning that teachers can use as a focus for instruction during guided reading with ELL students (see Figure 5.4). This chart includes the NRP's five components of reading, and we have added our "plus" components, high-frequency words, vocabulary, language structures, text selection, and arching over all instruction, a foundation of background knowledge. By always giving attention to the students' existing background knowledge, teachers are able to use the spiraling sequence of instruction we discussed in Chapter 1.

FIGURE 5.4. Guided Reading Components—English Language Learners

Oral Language	Fluency	Word Recognition Strategies
Phonics	High-Frequency Words	Comprehension
Vocabulary	Language Structures	Text Selection

GUIDED READING FOR ELL STUDENTS WITHOUT NATIVE LANGUAGE INSTRUCTION

In guided reading with ELL students, teachers need to address the components discussed above. In this section and the next, we present general ideas about how to differentiate reading instruction according to age level and whether or not students are receiving instruction in their native language. In the Appendix at the end of the book, Tables A.1 and A.2 provide specific instructional strategies based on students' identified needs at two age levels.

K–2 ELL Students

Build on. Keeping in mind that grouping is done according to language proficiency, when teachers plan for small-group instruction or guided reading for primary ELL students, they need to go beyond identifying the students' reading level. Teachers need to observe the students' language production, including, but not limited to, their pronunciation of the words. During nonthreatening, small-group or individual conversations about books, teachers can gather information on language development and reading skills. They also need to look for what students comprehend and where the gaps are in their understanding (vocabulary, idiomatic expressions, unfamiliar situations, etc.).

Explain and Involve. Teachers can use the gathered information for further instruction. Providing hands-on experiences in which students become involved in interesting activities is important to help them develop the vocabulary and grammar they need to understand English texts. "Live" experiences help students bridge background knowledge they already have with the English language they need. Such experiences also can expand and enhance their existing background knowledge, helping them to build more conceptual understandings, which leads to further vocabulary and grammar acquisition, which leads to better comprehension of texts. It is a wonderful, spiraling learning cycle (see Figure 5.5).

When working with ELL students with more limited English, the teacher can allow the children to talk about the book in their native language. We need to remember that children comprehend a language before they are able to speak it. When children develop

Figure 5.5. Aspects to Consider When Reading with K–2 Students

- When doing picture walks, point at the pictures when you are talking.
- Make sure students know the meaning of important content words before reading: nouns, verbs, and adjectives.
- Read a sentence together to help students hear how it should sound.
- With new arrivals, avoid questions such as, "what do you see? Find the . . . ." They might be able to do this, but may not have enough English to understand or respond to the questions.
- Problem solve together appropriate words for a sentence; always challenge them at a level that moves them forward in vocabulary and concept development.
- Teach students to try out two different words to see which works better for the sentence; refer to context and illustrations, not "what sounds right."
- Ask students what strategy (having taught and modeled them during shared reading) can be used to figure out the word.
- If a student is stuck on a word, skip that word and ask the student if he or she knows the meaning of the whole sentence. If so, have the student explain.
- Ask a student to name all the items in the picture or tell what is happening in the picture to facilitate problem solving words or comprehension.
- Ask a student to think of a word that he or she knows that might fit with the meaning of the sentence.
- Stop in strategic places and work with the group to summarize the text.
- For words with multiple meanings, ask, "Why is the author using this word if it means . . . ?"
- Model through "think alouds" how you think about text meaning and problem solve unknown words.

language, their thinking is more sophisticated than their oral production. Therefore, if the teacher allows them to speak in their native language about the book they read in English, children are able to develop and articulate their ideas at a higher level than they can in English (Nathenson-Mejía, 1989). When children talk with one another about books in their native language, they have the opportunity to express their ideas without the pressure of putting words into English. Students can get the satisfaction of discussion at an intelligent level. This also helps them prepare their ideas for a discussion in English.

This practice not only provides a comfort level for the children but at the same time builds trust between the children and the teacher. If the teacher speaks the children's language, these conversations can be used to diagnose how much comprehension students have. If the teacher is not bilingual, he or she may be able to find an older student in the school or an adult in the classroom or school who speaks the children's language. If so, the teacher can be given a general idea of their conversation and the students' understanding of and ideas about the text. If this language support is not available, the teacher can ask the children to draw the different events of the story. By watching how they create the drawings and listening to how they explain them, the teacher will be able to see how much comprehension the children have.

Grades 3–5 ELL Students

Build on. Guided reading groups are an excellent opportunity to help intermediate English Language Learners improve their language and their reading ability. Older students need all the same supports as younger students, but they also need more (see Figure 5.6). In small-group instruction, students are able to demonstrate what they comprehend about a reading. As pointed out previously, often ELL students *do* comprehend subtleties of a text but are unable to communicate what they understand because of their limited oral language proficiency. This may result in their being placed in a reading group that does not really meet their needs.

FIGURE 5.6. Aspects to Consider When Reading with Grades 3–5 Students (in Addition to Those Covered in Figure 5.8)

- Small-group instruction is an excellent opportunity to listen to students' oral proficiency in English, their use of the structure of the English language, and their fluency with the academic English they are able to use.
- Information gained during small-group instruction will help the teacher identify areas of need for mini-lessons that may benefit a variety of students.
- The conversation between teacher and students during the lesson will reinforce the students' language production, model the use of academic English, and support students' efforts to talk about a specific topic based on the text being read. All of this also will reinforce the vocabulary and grammar structures being developed.

Explain and Involve. Summarizing and retelling are tools that require students to push their understanding of text to identify and explain the main point and supporting details, whether orally or in writing (Marzano et al., 2004). By working on summaries and re-tellings in reading groups, teachers can help ELL students identify and understand the different text structures and can support their oral development as they talk about the text.

Using graphic organizers and pictures helps students visualize the elements of the story, making them more tangible and thus easier to place in order and talk about. While filling out graphic organizers together, the teacher can encourage and support talk about the text, text features, and text structures. Once the graphic organizer is complete, it can be used to support both summarizing (brief) and retellings (extended) and help students see the difference between them. There are many existing graphic organizers for students to use when learning about storytelling elements and sequence. However, many of these have a nonlinear organization in order to make them more interesting and attractive. This can be confusing for ELL students who are being asked to learn the linear style of retelling required by U.S. schools. Therefore, we recommend that teachers use graphic organizers and storyboards that are simple and linear in nature (see Figure 5.7). This makes the retelling expectations very clear to students and will help them as they learn to put their ideas together in ways that will fulfill the requirements for reading assessments.

FIGURE 5.7. Story Mapping Graphic Organizer—Linear

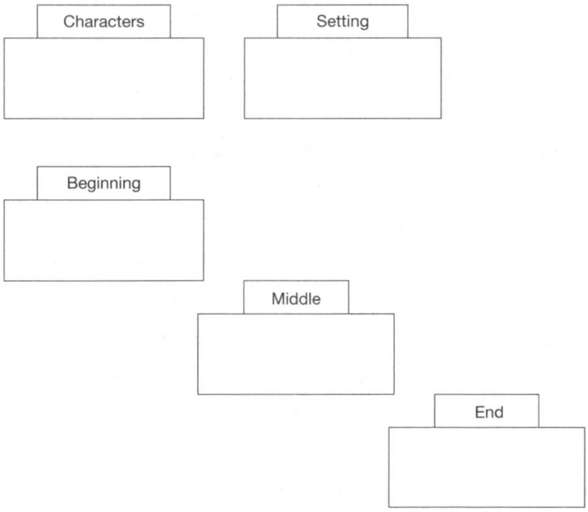

In addition, we suggest using the self-monitoring section at the end of Table A.2 in the Appendix. Students can begin to look at their own learning process and see how their abilities change over time. They can set goals, have a plan for reaching those goals, and consider what worked and what didn't when reviewing their learning. This self-monitoring process should be done with guidance from the teacher, but also with continual movement toward greater independence.

GUIDED READING FOR ELL STUDENTS WITH NATIVE LANGUAGE INSTRUCTION

K–2 ELL Students

Build on. ELL students who are emergent literacy learners in both a native language and English need very explicit and careful instruction. Literacy instruction in English should *build on* what they are learning about reading and writing in their native language. The teachers can decide how to arrange guided reading in their classroom; however, it is important that students receive literacy instruction in both languages all the time. Small-group instruction in their second language is most effective when it is built from students' native language; therefore, teachers should not wait until the students develop one language to teach the other (Uribe, 2004). The same techniques teachers use in the primary language may be of benefit in the second language, although they need to focus more on oral language development since most of the phonetics will come through conversations.

Explain and Involve. Allowing the children to interact in their native language during English instruction has definite benefits for students' comprehension and native language development; however, the teacher needs be careful about this and prevent long-term dependence on this interaction throughout the school year. Children need to gradually move toward using more English according to each child's comfort level and proficiency in the second language. Some children would like to continue with native language conversation for too long, and this will prevent them from developing oral language abilities in English. For some children, it will take 1, 2, or 3 months; for others, it may take longer. The important factor is that the teacher provides the comfort level to interact in the child's native language only as long as considered necessary. Then the teacher begins to move the child toward using more and more English in these guided and supported conversations. For some children, this means that by March or April they will be able to hold the entire discussion in English. For others, in March or April they may be only at 70%, but it will be evident that they have come a long way since September when their entire conversation was in the native language. Because they also are receiving guided reading in the native language, students have the opportunity to interact and develop the native language at a higher level, which will benefit their English development over time.

Grades 3–5 ELL Students

Build on. The major focus of small-group instruction in the intermediate levels should be on comprehension, vocabulary development, and English oral expression and structures. Students may be literate in their native language either because they have received instruction in both languages here in the United States, or because they were already literate in their native language when they arrived. Whichever is the case, their reading level is usually at or close to grade level, and they have a variety of academic experiences. Therefore, a focus on comprehension and high-order thinking should be the priority for their reading time.

Explain and Involve. Conversation about books that also scaffolds content and language builds trust between the teacher and the students. Such conversations help the teacher individualize instruction and teach and reinforce the skills the children need to work on.

Having the students in small settings and grouped according to language proficiency allows the teacher to conduct effective small-group instruction. Most often the skill an individual student needs to work on is a skill the whole group will benefit from. Teachers can scaffold a high level of conversation about text and content, getting the students involved in critical thinking about the books and their own reading strategies.

CHOOSING TEXTS FOR GUIDED READING

We would like to stress again that texts should be chosen according to children's ages and not according to their reading level. Although it may be tempting to give a 3rd grader who speaks no English the book that goes, "The bear is brown. The bear is white. The bear is black," teachers must resist. Older students are not pleased to be given "baby" books, and their motivation for learning will wither quickly. Teachers should use more age-appropriate texts and take time to scaffold and shelter the content during all phases of literacy instruction. The time they spend helping students in age-appropriate ways will pay off in motivation and higher level thinking.

Texts that the teacher selects for guided reading might be the same ones used during read alouds or shared reading, or they might be new to the students to help them work on problem solving new vocabulary. They also could be familiar texts that the teacher uses to review concepts, review mini-lessons, or respond to literature. Texts can be fiction books (picture books or chapter books), news articles, student-level newspapers or magazines, informational books, poems, songs—just about anything that is high quality and age appropriate. When choosing texts for guided reading, teachers need to look for texts with the characteristics listed in Figure 5.8.

FIGURE 5.8. Text Selection for Guided Reading

Look for texts that

- Develop and scaffold language acquisition
- Provide opportunities for explicit and implicit meaning (literal and inferential)
- Provide language with opportunities for discussing and learning English language structures
- Have an important instructional value and are also attractive and inviting
- Use rich vocabulary and are well written
- Have a complex theme that is developmentally appropriate
- Have well-done illustrations that are appropriate to the text and support comprehension
- Include concepts students have some background knowledge about and whose vocabulary they might be familiar with
- Are appropriate for the grade level

ASSESSING GUIDED READING

Conferences are an effective tool for monitoring students' language development as well as their reading development. Teachers can use this time to assess students' use of English in response to a variety of genres and text levels. They also can model English language discourse structures that students will need to master. This section provides guidelines for teachers to use in structuring their conferences with ELL students and specifics to look for during conferences. We will discuss how these conferences look for new speakers of English and how they will change over time as students become more proficient with English.

In Chapter 2 we discussed how the daily schedule and the small-group reading instruction schedule might look in a classroom with English Language Learners. Taberski (2000) uses students' specific reading needs and pulls two or three students with the same needs together when scheduling a conference. However, our suggestion is to conduct conferences during the time teachers are doing small-group reading so all students in the group benefit from the conference conversation. (Since the students are grouped by language proficiency, the teaching point for a child helps all of the others in the group. As the teacher conferences with one student, the others are listening to the conversation.) We believe this format of doing an individual conference within a small-group setting will benefit ELL students more because it provides a wealth of aural and oral language development. In addition, it offers opportunities for the teacher to talk with the students more often about reading strategies and connect the reading lesson with the conference.

How to Organize Reading Conferences in Small Groups

Usually, small-group instruction has five to six children in a group. (We are aware that sometimes teachers have fewer or more children due the number of the students in the classroom and the time restraints for literacy.) Before beginning the lesson, the teacher has told the students to bring their book bags with them. Once the group is in place, the teacher begins with a conference. She has chosen a student who she feels needs a conference, one who has requested a conference, or the next person on her running list for conferencing. She conducts the conference for 10 minutes, focusing on what that student needs. After the conference, the rest of the small-group time can be a regular guided reading session.

During the conference the teacher may talk with the student briefly about what he or she has read, ask the student to read orally a selection of the text (while the teacher takes notes or does a running record), or ask the student to do a retelling or summary of the reading. Following the activity, teacher and student discuss what he or she is doing well and identify something to work on and what strategy to use.

The next day the teacher chooses another student in the group, and so on. By the end of the week the teacher has conferenced with four or five students in every reading group. By the end of 2 weeks of instruction the teacher has had individual conferences with all of the students in the class. If teachers follow this pattern for 4 weeks, they might then take a week off from conferences and focus small-group time on strategy instruction needed by everyone in the reading group. At the end of 5 weeks they will have conferenced with each student twice and worked as a group for a whole week, and the conference cycle can begin again.

Another way to do conferences is to take 2 days a week and conference with three students in the group. The teacher listens and takes notes on each student's needs. If everyone needs to work on the same strategy, the teacher can provide a strategy mini-lesson right there that will help all of them and that they can practice independently. If they have different strategy needs, the teacher can use that information to pull together small groups at another time for targeted instruction.

Embedding the conferences within the guided reading lesson provides direct instruction for students more often. We consider this necessary for ELL students since they are developing not only reading skills but also vocabulary, oral language, and comprehension. In addition, the students need the oral interaction with academic language more often; if they don't have the opportunity to talk at an academic level, it will be hard for them to become fluent in the language of school and understand the texts. We need to remember that this is an opportunity to practice and apply academic English. Because everyone in the group is at the same language proficiency level and similar (although not necessarily exactly the same) age and reading levels, this is a nonthreatening environment in which they can feel safe using their developing academic language skills.

What to Look for When Assessing Guided Reading

When teachers assess during guided reading, they often do running records and analyze them using three cueing systems—meaning (semantics), visual (grapho-phonetics), and structure (syntax). In addition, we suggest other areas for teachers to assess during guided reading, such as using prepositions, using language background knowledge, and paying attention to English language structures. The checklist in Table 5.1 can help teachers remember to focus on these areas for ELL students while at the same time helping them keep track of their students' progress.

TABLE 5.1. Assessing Guided Reading

Behaviors	No Evidence	Sometimes	Often
1. Fluently reads prepositions, conjunctions, and articles			
2. Differentiates language rules between L1 and L2 (if applicable)			
3. Uses known words to read unknown words			
4. Uses illustration clues to self-correct or figure out the words			
5. Uses language syntax (grammar) to self-correct			
6. Uses self-correction when substitution and omission occur			
7. Uses language structures to self-correct or figure out words			
8. Uses phonics patterns to read unknown words			
9. Recognizes essential meaning of the sentences and re-reads			
10. Identifies story elements			
11. Uses punctuation to build fluency			
12. Uses intonation to ensure the meaning of the text			

SUMMARY

Guided reading or small-group instruction is the final teacher-support component in the literacy block before independent reading. For ELL students, this time is when they learn about language and pull together their learning from all three components of reading instruction. We consider the following basic principles important for guided reading for all ELL students, no matter their age or language proficiency:

- Group children according to language proficiency and age groups
- Provide daily guided reading groups to check for students' understandings of the concepts taught during read alouds and shared reading
- Provide language development instruction according to students' English language proficiency (don't assume all ELL students of the same age need the same instruction)
- Provide the structure of the language as well as the meaning
- Challenge and support students' reading of high-level texts and their use of high-level oral language. Don't keep learning at a surface or "easy" level; students need to continually increase their proficiencies.
- Connect reading to what students know from their native language, oral and written
- Focus on comprehension instead of pronunciation (you can work on pronunciation at other times)
- Use reading conferences to assess ELL students' strengths and needs in both language and reading

Guided reading is the point at which teachers help ELL students pull together everything they have been learning about language and reading in English during read aloud and shared reading. Teachers can support students through guided reading while at the same time letting them have more control over the reading experience. This will better prepare them to be successful during independent reading.

CHAPTER 6

Writing Instruction: Developing Literacy

Sally writes: *Writing down my ideas makes me nervous. As I begin to write this chapter, I worry about how the audience will receive my ideas. Will I be able to express myself in a way that communicates my message effectively?*

What I don't worry about is being able to use the language, English, to write what I want to say. I don't worry about grammar, or spelling, or punctuation. I know how to put the words together so they make sense.

If I were writing in Spanish, my second language, everything would be different. Although I have been speaking, reading, and writing in Spanish for 30 years, when I write in Spanish, I mostly think in English. The words in my head are Spanish, but the way I construct the ideas is based on English, even though I know the rules for grammar, spelling, and punctuation in Spanish. When I write in Spanish, I worry about the mechanics and the ideas; it can be very stressful.

It is easy to think of my foundation of language in English as interfering *with my ability to write in Spanish, instead of the idea that my English* influences *my Spanish writing. This perspective doesn't hurt me, personally, since when I write in Spanish I am not being graded and I know where to go to get help. But for a student in school, trying to learn to read and write in a new language while, at the same time, learning to speak and understand this new language, learning academic content in the new language, and* becoming accustomed to a new culture, the situation is different. It can be devastating for a student when a teacher looks at native language as interfering with rather than influencing learning.*

NO MATTER HOW OLD they are or how much schooling they have or haven't had, all students bring with them knowledge about how to use their native language to communicate. Teachers must recognize and *build on* this knowledge in a positive way. If teachers put away the idea of interference and replace it with an understanding of how a student's native language influences learning

---

WHAT WE KNOW

Goodman and Wilde (1992) and a team of researchers did a 2-year study with Tohono O'odham children in southern Arizona. Although these Native American children were native English speakers, they came from a complex, linguistically and culturally diverse community. This in-depth look at the writing of 3rd and 4th graders yielded a set of principles that can be used by all teachers to guide instructional design for bringing out the best in children through writing. These principles remind us that children learn about writing through engaging in writing in an encouraging social environment, and children need to learn to express themselves through many modalities of writing.

---

to write in English, they will be better able to help their students develop confidence and competence as writers in English.

In writing, as in reading, it is essential that teachers create direct connections between what students know and what is new. Teachers can help students recognize what they are able to do and what they need to learn, and base that new learning on what they already know how to do, continuing the spiraling instruction process.

In this chapter we will look at what ELL students bring with them to the writing experience and how that information can help teachers design appropriate writing instruction for ELL students. After explaining the value of teaching nonfiction writing, we will discuss writing instruction for all ELL students and also some specifics for those children who have some writing background in their native language. Finally, we will look at various aspects of assessing students' writing in order to inform instruction.

UNDERSTANDING HOW LANGUAGE WORKS

Once children have learned that language is used for communication, that it has oral and written forms, and that it is made up of various sounds that signify meanings and symbols that correspond to these meanings and sounds, these concepts do not have to be relearned in a new language. If children have experience and vocabulary for food and cooking, then they don't need to relearn what food and cooking are all about. What they need in the new language is vocabulary and print knowledge (linking known meanings to new words, both oral and written), syntax (figuring out how to put the new words together), and pragmatics (the purposes and expectations in the new culture). Teachers can use the cueing systems to help them understand what children know about language (see Table 6.1). Remember that just because they know these things, doesn't mean they can explain them; this is *tacit* knowledge, or schemata about language.

Semantics

The foundation for writing is *semantics*, or meaning. Without meaning, there is no point to language, whether oral or written. Children learn language because there is a payoff, communication, which leads to getting one's needs met. All of this is based on meaning. Even children who do not have extensive vocabularies and concept development, have basic knowledge of how language

TABLE 6.1. What Students May Know About Their Native Language

Semantics	Syntax	Grapho-phonetics	Pragmatics
Understandings ELL students may have about the world of literacy	Knowledge of how their native language works (L1)	Knowledge of how language sounds and looks	Understanding home/school expectations
• Vocabulary: about home, school, the world, literature (songs, rhymes, books, stories) • Knowing that meaning can be created and communicated through print • Schemata about how literacy in the world works, including signs, logos, etc. • Schemata about the use of writing to communicate • Schemata about oral and written discourse	• What sounds "right" • Tense conjugations • Pronoun usage • Gender distinctions • Verb irregularities • Use of adverbs, adjectives • Use of size and amount descriptors • Word order	• Recognizing sounds of native language • Producing sounds of native language • Recognizing native language in print (various fonts and formats) • Recognizing the relationship between sound and print • Producing native language in print	• What is the value and place of language in *my* home life? • What is the value and place of literacy and school in *my* home life? • What does *my* home expect my behavior in school to be? • What does the school expect my behavior in school to be?

works and can use their native language to communicate. If they know how to recognize and perhaps write their names, then they have the beginnings of understandings about print—that it carries meaning, it can communicate.

Syntax

How language puts itself together, *syntax,* comes across as tacit knowledge for children. The explicit rules of grammar are meaningless for most children. For example, native Spanish-speaking children rarely make mistakes in the use of gender (*la mesa, el caballo*), the use of *to be* verbs (*ser/estar*), or the placement of adjectives (*la camisa roja*). Without thinking, a 4-year-old native Spanish speaker could say:

> *La camisa roja esta en la mesa y el caballo blanco es de mi papá.*
> (The red shirt is on the table, and the white horse is my
>   father's.)

Seems simple enough, but consider: There is gender agreement among the articles, the adjectives, and the nouns (*roja* with *la camisa* and *blanco* with *el caballo*). There is a distinction between one use of "to be" (*estar*) for a temporary state of being (the shirt being on the table) and the other use of "to be" (*ser*) for a more permanent state of being (the horse belonging to father). All are rather sophisticated linguistic concepts.

This is why Chukovsky (1963) called children "linguistic geniuses," as any 4-year-old can do this in his/her native language. Teachers of English Language Learners must recognize that English syntax is different from that of ELL students' native language, which means learning to think differently about how to put ideas together. This takes specific instruction, modeling through shared writing, time, and lots of practice.

When children are acquiring literacy in both languages, the concepts of syntax need to be taught explicitly so they will be able to see the differences and similarities in the languages.

Grapho-phonetics

The *grapho-phonetic* system is really made up of two parts: the graphics or symbols of the language and the phonetics, or sounds, of the language. Grapho-phonetics puts the two systems together so that language can be written down by authors and writing can be interpreted by readers. Children who can speak and understand when spoken to have basic knowledge of their native language's phonetic system. They have developed enough ability to distinguish and use the sounds for effective oral communication. Their knowledge of the graphic system, or written language, will vary greatly, however, depending on their age, the language they speak, and the importance their culture places on learning written language. Children who cannot read in their native language may still recognize that print is an aspect of language that carries meaning and communicates. Here again, it is imperative that teachers take the time to find out what children know and understand about how language works.

Teachers need to *build on* the students' own foundation of sounds and their knowledge of language symbols (print) and help them distinguish between the sounds and print in their native and new languages. It is helpful for children to learn about the sounds that transfer between their language and English, those that partially transfer, and those that will be new for them.

Pragmatics

Often overlooked is the *pragmatics* of both writing and reading, but it affects us all greatly. Situations, expectations, and purpose come under the pragmatics system. We make decisions about how much attention we should pay to a task based on pragmatics: Are we interested in it, will it be on a test, do we want to please the parent or teacher who set us to the task? Children come to school with various understandings of the pragmatics surrounding literacy and schooling. They have notions about the role and value of literacy and schooling in their lives. If we don't take the time to find out what these notions are, we may make erroneous assumptions that will inhibit the creation of constructive relationships between students, teachers, and families.

For example, Aresani's family has been in the United States for about 2 years. Her father has two jobs, and her mother has one. Aresani's teacher knows, from conversations with the child and her parents, that they don't buy books or frequent the library, and the teacher has concluded that literacy is not overly important in this family. However, what the teacher has not realized is that quite a bit of literacy is going on at home, just not around books. Aresani's parents read the Spanish newspaper, they use the Spanish language yellow pages frequently, and there are always Spanish language magazines around the house, brought from Mexico. Her parents pay bills, write grocery lists, and read letters from family. Aresani and her siblings attend Sunday School and go to church with their parents. Aresani's mother hopes that her daughter will finish high school and go on to a small community college. Reading and writing is going on all the time in their home, and Aresani's parents expect that literacy will play an important role in their children's lives. The teacher needs to uncover these expectations in order to truly understand Aresani and to be able to help her reach her goals.

Pragmatics also includes knowledge of the discourse structures and the cultural backgrounds of the children. The various genre structures in English are often quite different from many ELL students' native language/culture experiences. One example is persuasive writing. In many countries, including Asian and Latino ones, children are not allowed to persuade an adult, let alone an authority figure such as a school principal. Sometimes we use "persuade the principal" as a prompt for learning persuasive writing. The vocabulary, the respect, and the language required to write such a piece is not something that comes easily for children from these cultures. We need to be aware of what children's expectations are before asking them to write in a specific genre.

WHY TEACH NONFICTION WRITING TO ELL STUDENTS?

With the high academic demands of schools in the 21st century, ELL students need to have a wide repertoire of strategies and language to produce a well-done piece of writing. Let us look at how some of the characteristics of nonfiction writing may support writing performance for ELL students. In nonfiction writing, students write for different audiences and many different purposes, such as informing, reporting, comparing, and analyzing (Stead, 2001). Nonfiction writing is more than writing a social studies report; it includes genre and styles such as personal narratives, personal descriptions, scientific explanations, directions, debates, evaluations, cards, recipes, poetry, compare and contrast, analysis, critiques, and much

> **WHAT WE KNOW**
>
> In a brief written for the Center for Performance Assessment by Reeves (2003a), there is an indication that children made great gains in their academic achievement when teachers focused on nonfiction writing. In addition, research by Amaral and Garrison (2002) that focused specifically on instruction with ELL students has shown that content instruction benefits ELL students' academic achievement.

more (Calkins, 1994; Graves, 1989). These various modes of writing help ELL students to acquire the English language, the language registers (audiences' purposes), and the literacy skills to produce an expected piece for their grade level.

Writing that expresses their growing sense of self and their identity allows students to map out where they have come from and where they are going (Cummins, 1999). They also engage in what Harklau (1999) calls "cultural inquiry through writing" (p. 125). As students move through the process of prewriting, drafting, revising, and editing for the different types of nonfiction writing, they learn that each requires a specific purpose and a specific audience. If ELL students are taught to develop a writing piece, taking into consideration their background, culture, and the cultural context for their writing, the pieces they produce will meet the expected academic requirements. In addition, writing nonfiction pieces will help ELL students understand their own perspectives on life in relationship to the new culture and the new language. Writing is the most powerful process for helping ELL students make a transition into culture and literacy in English.

WRITING INSTRUCTION IN ENGLISH: CONNECTING THE READING AND WRITING PROCESSES

Build on. As we have seen, how we approach writing instruction depends on how much ELL students already know about writing in their own language and how much oral English they have. But no matter what they already know, or don't know, instruction should begin with something that is familiar to them. Encourage students to write about what they know:

- Themselves and their families, the holidays they celebrate, favorite foods
- Where they came from, traveling to the United States
- The work their families do or did before
- What they are interested in and their favorite activities
- Their frustrations, questions, and fears, and what they are unsure about

Throughout writing instruction, direct connections should be made back to reading instruction. Concept development and oral language development are essential components of good writing, and both are developed through the various components of reading instruction. Being exposed to high-quality literature is also important, as it provides models for how written English works. High expectations for success, along with acceptance of approximations and supportive scaffolding to help students continually improve, are additional essential elements of good instruction for ELL students.

Explain and Involve. An effective way to incorporate all of this is through thematic teaching, as discussed in Chapter 2. Finding a familiar theme for students to work on, such as families, food, cities, or farms (depending on the students' backgrounds), allows teachers to immerse students in a comfortable concept. Through the use of realia, literature, guest speakers, and discussions, students can acquire the oral vocabulary in English that corresponds with their topic knowledge. Teachers can use these opportunities to make direct connections to the vocabulary in print and help students begin to write about these topics in English. Stories using the language experience approach can help to model both oral English and written English. Interactive writing, shared writing, guided writing, and paired writing experiences will help to further scaffold students' writing in English. Teachers can conference with pairs of students who are writing together to help them gain confidence and knowledge about writing in English. All of this will help students as they begin to write individually. Planning the writing curriculum so that it *builds on* what is being covered in reading will facilitate learning for the students and help them see the direct connections between writing and reading (Kendal & Khuon, 2006). (See Table 6.2.)

TABLE 6.2. Connecting Reading and Writing Instruction

Reading Instruction	Skills Block	Writing Instruction
Comprehension: Ex: visualization	Sentence structure: Ex: descriptions	Author style and purpose: Ex: creating images
Story structure: Beginning, middle, end	Language structure: Beginning, middle, end	Story structure: Beginning, middle, end
Genre: Elements of particular genre	Genre Structures	Genre-based language used to express ideas
Story Elements: Characters, setting, conflict, resolution	Descriptive language	Story elements: Characters, setting, conflict, resolution
Vocabulary development: Vocabulary specific to topic or genre	Spelling: Phonics, word families, word parts, word origin study	Word choice: Finding "chili," "juicy," or "just right" words

For example, if the class is working on a household theme in reading and social studies, the instruction in writing can help review and solidify new vocabulary and help students see how to use the vocabulary to describe and write about familiar topics, for example, soap. Creating a "soaps" chart with the students will help make this process explicit. Referring to the categories in the chart, students can begin by writing descriptions of what soaps are found in their homes, where they are found, and how they are used. From there, students can think of stories to tell that involve soap and can write a personal narrative. They also can come up with advertisements, write scripts for television commercials, and create posters for their own "brand" of soap. They can research the different kinds of soap used by classmates, different brands used in different countries, and so forth. They can investigate the ingredients in soap, do a history timeline of soap, even explore the process of soap manufacturing and distribution. A simple discussion about soap can lead to large increases in concept development, vocabulary development, reading proficiency, and writing abilities.

NATIVE LANGUAGE WRITING INSTRUCTION

One approach to teaching ELL students to become capable writers in English is to encourage them to begin by writing in their native language. In this section we will explore this approach for both students who are not receiving native language instruction and those who are.

Writing for ELL Students Without Native Language Instruction

Build on. Why would a teacher who speaks only English want her students to write in their native languages? What advantage would there be in having students write stories and personal narratives that the teacher could not read? The advantages are numerous, from ease of expression to personal pride, to using students' writing as orientation and assessment texts. Having students write in their native languages adds dimension and diversity to a classroom and teaches all students more about languages and how they work (Nathenson-Mejía, 1992). (See Figure 6.1.)

Not being able to communicate easily is a very frustrating experience for students, at any age; remember the analogy of the basketball being pushed through a keyhole? When children have the opportunity to talk and write in their native language in school, they are able to express ideas at a much more complex and interesting level than when they write in English, even if they have had a few years of English instruction in school. Opportunities to speak and write in one's native language help to relieve some of the frustration of not being able to communicate effectively in English.

It is important that second language learners see themselves as smart and capable. Too often students learning English feel that there is so much they don't know and can't do, they forget (and sometimes their teachers forget) how much they do know and are

FIGURE 6.1. Why Have Students Write in Their Native Language?

Opportunities to write in their native language helps students with:

1. Ability to express ideas in familiar language
2. Learning conventions of written language in a familiar format (with help from native speakers)
3. Value and pride in using native language
4. Learning to use English to talk about what they wrote
5. Teaching nonspeakers a few words
6. Learning the importance of public display and publishing texts for use by other students

capable of. Opportunities to write in their native language can give students a sense of pride and accomplishment. Having teachers and other students recognize their abilities, even if they can't read the writing, helps reinforce this pride. Students who believe they are capable and have something to offer are more willing and able to learn.

English learners can use their native language writing as a platform for improving their oral proficiency in English. Students can use the ideas they have written down to begin learning vocabulary and phrasing in English in order to talk about and share with their classmates what they have written. The English vocabulary they learn will be based on concepts they already know, thus making it meaningful. Hopefully, their desire to communicate effectively will motivate regular attempts to share verbally. At the same time, English learners can teach their classmates a few words in their native language, reinforcing their pride in being able to speak the language.

Involve. One of the most difficult situations for teachers of English Language Learners is the lack of materials in the students' native languages, especially content materials. It is difficult to help students keep up their content knowledge when there are few science or social studies materials available in their languages. However, students themselves can create texts for other students to read, providing informal content texts as well as general orientation texts. With the availability and ease of digital cameras, computers, and printers, students can take photographs, create texts in a variety of language fonts, and easily print small books to help new students learn about their school, *"Todo acerca de la escuela primaria, Goldrick"* ("All about Goldrick Elementary"), or books about content such as *"Todo de los lagartos"* ("All about lizards"). In creating these texts, students are engaged in the complete writing process, learning to plan and organize, compose, revise, and edit their writing for a real audience. They are able to publish their work, knowing it will be used and appreciated.

Cooperation across schools will make this most effective. A school with a large Spanish-speaking population can create a variety of texts in Spanish, taking advantage of older students and community members to help with editing. These materials can be shared with other schools that may have only a few Spanish-speaking students. This also will work with other language communities, for example, a school with a sizeable Vietnamese community (or Somalian, or Russian) can create materials in Vietnamese and share them with other schools. A truly ambitious school district can create a Web site where these materials can be stored and downloaded when needed.

Writing for ELL Students with Native Language Instruction

Build on and Explain. Children who have received or are receiving native language instruction use the phonetics that they learned in the early stages of their literacy development, just as native English speakers use the phonetics they know when they are emergent writers.

Students who walk into classrooms able to communicate verbally in their native language have basic knowledge about how their language works. If they also can recognize and write their own name in their native language, then they have beginning knowledge about written language.

If students have some knowledge related to the cueing systems in their native language, they can start to adapt that knowledge into their second language. For example, if young students can point at each word when they read in Spanish, then they have the conceptual knowledge about print to begin reading books at their comprehension level in English. If they can recognize and write the beginning sounds of words in Spanish, they can begin to recognize and use familiar sound patterns in English. If they know that they can use color words to describe something in Spanish, they can begin to learn color words and use them to describe things in English. By constantly connecting one language with the other, children will be building the two languages at the same time. Although we do not advocate teaching both languages within the same lesson, separate lessons in English that *build on* knowledge students have in Spanish provide the language foundation they need as teachers *explain* what they need to learn in English. This process can, and should, begin in kindergarten!

During this stage, native English-speaking children use invented spelling based on their own pronunciations in an attempt to write stories and make their written language comprehensible.

Children who are working in both languages will use invented spelling based on their pronunciations and knowledge of both of their languages. They will use the phonics and structure of the language they know, and will try to make sense of the story based on their native language and background knowledge (Nathenson-Mejía, 1989). For example, Spanish-speaking students may write:

> Sam fish hav sharp tis.   *or*   Sme fish have srp tids.

In the two versions of "Some fish have sharp teeth," we can see that each child had different understandings of the vowels in *some*. One child interpreted his pronunciation of *some* as using the sound /ä/ (as in *father*) (pronunciation symbols guide from the *New Oxford American Dictionary*, 2001), and the other child skipped that vowel altogether, but remembered the *e* at the end of the word. One child may have made the connection between the /SH/ sound in the familiar word *fish* and the /SH/ sound in *sharp*. The other child did not. Both children may have had difficulty pronouncing *teeth* because of the /TH/, which is not used in Spanish. However, both children interpreted their pronunciation of *ee* (/ē/) as needing the letter *i*, most likely because *i* in Spanish is *always* pronounced /ē/.

It is imperative that teachers identify right away what children know and can do in writing both their native language and English. Using this information, teachers can *build on* these strengths in order to *explain* and extend the students' conceptual and linguistic knowledge. Research has shown that much of our conceptual knowledge is transferable from one language to another (Cummins, 1981). Once we know what a cow is in the United States, we don't need to relearn the concept of cow when we go to India. We *do* need to learn a new way to say, read, and write "cow" (linguistic knowledge) *and* we may need to learn new ideas about how cows are regarded and treated (cultural and pragmatic knowledge), but the basic concept of the animal is the same.

Table 6.3 shows which sounds from English are found also in Spanish. (If your students speak another language, you can find similar resources on the Internet that provide this information.) Talking about these sounds with students while doing shared and interactive writing activities will help them learn and remember

TABLE 6.3. Sounds from English and Their Relationship to Spanish

English to Spanish	Grapho-phonetics in English
Transfer	• Consonant sounds: B, F, K, L, M, N, P, S, T, W, V, Z • D (initial) • C (hard and soft) • Blends: BL, CL, FL, GL, PL, BR, CR, DR, FR, GR, TR • Digraphs: CH • G (hard) • Rhyming words • Alphabetizing
Partial Transfer	• D (middle/ending)
No Transfer	• Short vowels and long vowels • J, H, Q, R, Y, G (soft) • Vowel combinations: AI, AY, AU, AW, AR, ER, EI, OO, OU, UR • Schwa: *ABOUT, LEMON, OFTEN* • Initial S: SC, SL, SN, SM, SP, SQ, ST, SCR, SPL, SPR, STR • Consonant blends and digraphs: SH, SH, SCH, SK, SW, TW, WH, SHR • Voiced and unvoiced: CK, GN, IGH, KN, NG, MB, PH, TCH, UGH, WR, WH, CH (Christmas) • Diagraphs except for CH

Adapted from various sources by the Denver Public Schools (Venturini & Uribe, 2003).

which sounds they can use from Spanish and which they need to modify for English. For example, although the /s/ sound is the same in the two languages, when /s/ comes at the beginning of the word in Spanish, it must be preceded by an *e* (/e/ as in *men*). Thus, we have words such as *español, escuela,* and *escribir.* Children learning English from Spanish may (and often do) write *espider* for *spider* because this small bit of phonetic knowledge is firmly embedded in how they use language. Just telling or reminding students is not enough. It may take many months of talking about the language differences while writing in English to embed the new form, and then we may see some overgeneralization, such as writing "specially" for "especially" in English. They might even begin to use the rule when writing in Spanish, leaving out the initial *e* in some words.

ASSESSING WRITING TO INFORM INSTRUCTION

Assessing Native Language Writing

Looking at students' writing in their native language will help a teacher understand their strengths and needs. Whatever a child is able to do with writing in either language, provides valuable information for the teacher (Escamilla & Coady, 2001). Assessment can be made of students' basic knowledge of directionality; the ability to write letters or characters; understanding what words are, phrasing, voice/print match, idea expression, and organization; and use of conventions. A native speaker can help assess students' writing to see what is conventional and what is "invented" (see Table 6.4). Such information tells the teacher what writing concepts the child already has that he or she may not be able to demonstrate in English.

Conducting an assessment of native language writing can help teachers understand what students know, even when they've been learning English for awhile. Often teachers are fooled by students' verbal dexterity, thinking they should know more about academic English than they are demonstrating, especially in writing, because

TABLE 6.4. Native Language Writing Assessment

What can the student do?	Notes from native language speaker	Notes from teacher
Use writing materials		
Write letters, numbers, characters		
Write words, with spacing		
Form sentences		
Use punctuation		
Write extended text		
Demonstrate syntax knowledge		
Put ideas into words		
Read back the writing in native language		
Explain about the writing in English		

they are able to converse easily. It is important to assess what they know about writing both in their native language and in English in order to help strengthen their writing in English.

As an example, let us look at a piece of writing from a 3rd grader, Rene, to assess what he knows about writing. A native Spanish speaker, Rene had been in the United States for a couple of years, and in this particular classroom all year. He was transcribing a nursery rhyme the way he remembered it, while some of his classmates looked on and convinced him to change his version to theirs.

Rene's version

Los cinco patitos se fueron a nadar. El mas pegueyito se ~~puso ayorar~~ guis quedar la mama enojada le guiso pegual porque patito se puso a yorar.

Corrected version in Spanish

Los cinco patitos se fueron a nadar. El más pequeñito se ~~puso a llorar~~ quiso quedar. La mamá se enojaba y le quiso pegar, Porque el patito se puso a llorar.

English translation

The five little ducks went to swim.
The littlest ~~began to cry~~ wanted to stay.
The mama got mad and wanted to spank him,
Because he began to cry.

Rene is an emerging writer. He certainly knows what writing is about and how to express his intentions through print, and he can take a poem he knows orally and transcribe it. He knows about sentences and the punctuation that defines them, although he is not consistent in its use. His spelling is inventive, following logical Spanish rules for orthography and pronunciation. He is influenced by the social nature of literacy; he understands revision and changed the wording of the poem when his comrades challenged his memory of this nursery rhyme.

The classroom teacher can gain valuable information from this piece. Rene should not be treated as if he knows nothing about writing, since it is clear that he has a great deal of knowledge. He can use help in spelling, which may signal a need for help with spelling in English as well. He needs to be more consistent in his use of capitals at the beginning of sentences. But since he has the conceptual knowledge of many important aspects of writing, his teacher can use this knowledge to help him begin to write effectively in English as well.

Assessing English Writing

When a student is being assessed for writing instruction, it is helpful to get a sense of what the child can write in English (see Table 6.5). It is important, however, for teachers to be sensitive about this, since being asked to write in a language one is learning can increase the anxiety of being assessed. The teacher can make it clear to students that they are not being tested, that no grade will be associated with this writing. It is a way for the teacher to learn what a student's strengths and needs are in English writing.

Let us look at an excerpt from Marta's writing in English. We can learn quite a bit about what Marta knows from her writing.

Marta's version

May tog ys japi and may jous an mi hsister en mi and mi mam en papo es cuing . . .

TABLE 6.5. English Language Writing Assessment

What can the student do?	Notes at entry to classroom	Notes after ___ months
Write letters, numbers, characters		
Use sound/symbol relationship		
Write words, with spacing		
Form sentences		
Use punctuation		
Write extended text		
Demonstrate syntax knowledge		
Put ideas into words		
Read the writing back in English		
Explain about the writing in English		

Corrected version

My dog is happy and my house and my sister and me and my mom and papa is coming . . .

Marta is a 2nd-grade native Spanish speaker who has been in U.S. schools for a couple of years. Her writing demonstrates strengths in both understanding and abilities, as well as needs in developing as a writer. She understands the basic conventions of sentence structure, beginning with a capital letter, using writing to talk about her family, and using "and" to keep a thought going. The spelling is strongly influenced by her pronunciation and knowledge of Spanish, as one can see from her use of *t* in *dog*, *j* in *happy* and *house*, and *y* in *is*. She definitely is experiencing some confusion around pronouncing and spelling *my* and *me*. This is understandable given the way *i* and *y* are pronounced in Spanish versus English. Working with Marta on the words *my, me, happy*, and *house* could go a long way toward helping her see the differences in how the two languages work. It would be most effective to work on these words in both her writing and reading at the same time to reinforce her developing ability and understanding.

Another aspect of Marta's writing that can use some support is the superficial nature of what she is writing. Her piece is essentially a list of family members; she continues on for three more lines repeating the list and stating that they are happy and they play together. It would be useful to know whether Marta can develop an idea in greater depth when talking or writing in Spanish, or whether this is her level of thinking and writing in both languages.

Even if students have been learning English 3, 4, or more years, it is still helpful to compare their writing in English with their native language writing. Often teachers make assumptions about the abilities of ELL students based only on their writing in their second language, which puts them at a distinct disadvantage (Escamilla & Coady, 2001). By comparing their writing in both languages, a teacher can see whether the strengths they demonstrate in native language writing are present in English writing and also whether the problems they have with writing are similar across the two languages. This assessment will help the teacher to determine the kind of instruction the child needs in each language.

In the example in Figure 6.2, Celia wrote two versions of a piece, one in her native language, Spanish, and one in English. Celia, a 3rd

FIGURE 6.2. Celia's Writing

Original version in Spanish:	Original version in English:
Cwando mi mama yama acomed tovos vajamos.	wen my mom cals time to eat we all cam doun
Corrected version in Spanish:	Corrected version in English:
Cuando mi mamá llama a comer, todos bajamos.	When my mom calls time to eat, we all come down.

grader, comes from a bilingual household, but all of her schooling has taken place in the United States. She is in a school that encourages the use of Spanish, but the school's goal is to move students into English as soon as possible. Therefore, she has had no formal or extensive instruction in writing in Spanish.

In both languages she is able to construct a meaningful sentence that creates an image in the mind of the reader. She is able to create this same image in two languages, no small feat! In Spanish, Celia understands opening and closing punctuation; she capitalizes the first word and includes a period at the end of the sentence. In English she is more challenged by these conventions; no capitals or periods are used at all. Perhaps she is unsure of how to do this in English; perhaps all her energy went into composing in English, and she wasn't able to pay attention to the mechanics at that moment. This is a good point for the teacher to explore and a way to help Celia understand the similarities in how sentences work in the two languages.

Most telling is her spelling in both languages. When children do not receive writing instruction in their native language, they must rely on their pronunciations of the words and what they know and remember about their native grapho-phonetic system. The back and forth influence between the two languages becomes very obvious in their writing (Nathenson-Mejía, 1989). Celia's spelling in Spanish contains common errors for children who are not immersed in Spanish print: *y* for *ll*, *d* for *r*, and *v* for *b*. She also has used an English character for a Spanish phoneme, *w* for *u*, which demonstrates the influence of English on her thinking, since *w* is not a character in the Spanish alphabet.

Her English spelling is actually quite good. She has left out the *h* in *when*, and the second *l* in *calls*, both silent letters. She has spelled *time* and *eat* correctly, which probably demonstrates her familiarity with these words from her reading and previous writing. Her spellings for *cam* (come) and *doun* (down) demonstrate her ability to match her pronunciation with what she knows about writing from Spanish. The letter *a* is always pronounced /ä/ as in "ah" in Spanish, and the English "silent e" rule is probably not one Celia has internalized yet, so she would pronounce *cam* as *come*. Her spelling of *doun* is a bit more complicated, since the letter *o* in Spanish is always /ō/ as in "go." Her use of *o* here may come from her memory of how the word *down* is spelled conventionally, or it may come from the way she is pronouncing the word, whereas her use of *u* follows Spanish pronunciation, /ōō/. Semantically she knows the word *down* and how to use it, but the grapho-phonetics of the word are difficult, and she has tried hard to make sense of it through her inventive spelling.

All of this information can help Celia's teacher assess her understanding of how the two languages work. The teacher can use this information to help Celia learn even more about the similarities and differences in the two languages, providing a foundation for further growth. Even more important, Celia's teacher can point out how much she *does* know, helping her to feel good about the knowledge she already has and confident about her potential to learn more. Instead of looking at her writing and seeing what she isn't doing, Celia, her teacher, and her parents can look at her writing to see what she *is* doing and set realistic goals for continued development.

Using Standards to Assess Writing

How do teachers assess ELL students in their writing in order to achieve academic standards? Based on the national standards for language arts (NCTE/IRA, 1996), assessing writing should have two main components. One is writing for different purposes, and the other is the mechanics of writing. When assessing ELL students in writing, teachers need to take into consideration that these are the two most difficult tasks for these students. As we mentioned before, the pragmatics that influence an individual's perspective on writing includes culture, discourse structures, semantics, the purpose for writing, and language development. The mechanics of writing is a compilation of the use, form, phonics, and language students need to know in order to compose writing that makes sense and is correct. Therefore, when teachers assess writing, they need to make sure that they have taught all of the above components in many different ways. Reeves, in his book *Making Standards Work* (2003b), talks about how teachers need to assess children continuously and also make sure that every time a concept is taught, students know that they are going to be assessed on it and how.

For example, if a 4th-grade teacher is teaching a 3-week unit on personal narrative, the students need to be told what is expected, how it will be taught, and how they will be assessed on the information (see possible standards to use in Figure 6.3). The first assessment is a preassessment of a story the students write; the purpose of the preassessment is to identify their strengths and weaknesses in the personal narrative style. The follow-up assessments will be based on the mini-lessons that address the indicators chosen from the standards. Using a scoring guide, students receive individual and/or group feedback that identifies the strengths and weaknesses in their story.

The final assessment will be divided into two parts. First the students will answer questions, based on the standards, about personal narrative fiction. The second part of the assessment will be the final piece of writing and it will include all the indicators on the scoring guide. It is important to work with the students to agree on how the points will be scored (what gets more points, and why) and which are the negotiable and non-negotiable tasks. Figure 6.4 shows an example of a final scoring guide to be used after teaching

---

FIGURE 6.3. Language Arts Standards That Can Apply to Personal Narratives

---

Standard 4. Students adjust their use of spoken, written, and visual language (e.g., conventions, style, vocabulary) to communicate effectively with a variety of audiences and for different purposes.

Standard 5. Students employ a wide range of strategies as they write and use different writing process elements appropriately to communicate with different audiences for a variety of purposes.

Standard 6. Students apply knowledge of language structure, language conventions (e.g., spelling and punctuation), media techniques, figurative language, and genre to create, critique, and discuss print and non-print texts.

(from NCTE/IRA, Standards for the English Language Arts, 1996)

FIGURE 6.4. Personal Narrative Writing—Scoring Guide

Name _____ Date_____	
Title of Writing _____	

	The topic is clear.
	I have a beginning, middle, and ending.
	Beginning has details that tell the audience what the story is about.
	I have a lead that makes the reader want to continue reading the story.
	There are supporting details in the middle.
	The details paint a picture in the reader's head.
	The story is sequenced correctly.
	Dialogue is used appropriately.
	The ending wraps up the story and ties in with the topic.
	Language mistakes have been corrected.
	There are paragraphs, and they are indented.
	There are transitions throughout the story and they are used appropriately.
	Handwriting is legible.
	Punctuation and capitalization are used correctly.
	There are spaces between words.
	The non-negotiable words are spelled correctly.
4	All above are checked.
3	Two or three elements are missing, but the piece makes sense.
2	Four or five elements are missing, and the piece doesn't always make sense.
1	Ideas, organization, and conventions all need to be improved.
0	Missing many elements on the list; piece is incomplete.

children all of the components of a personal narrative. Figure 6.5 is another example of a scoring guide, this one for expository writing, following a similar process. These scoring guides should be used by the students to self-assess their writing and then by the teacher for a final assessment. Ideally, once this assessment is complete, teacher and student will have a conference to review the results and set up future writing goals.

Writing to Prompts

Many state proficiency tests use prompts to assess children. A prompt is a very complex task for ELL students to interpret. The children need to understand exactly what the prompts are asking them to do. It helps if students have had a similar experience so they can draw on their own background knowledge. The students need to know what genre the prompt is asking for and how that genre is supposed to be written. Although this is true

FIGURE 6.5. Expository Writing—Scoring Guide

Name _____ Date_____	
Title of Writing _____	

	The topic is clear.
	I have an introduction, supporting details, and a conclusion.
	Introduction has details that tell the audience what the story is about.
	I have a lead that makes the reader want to continue reading the story.
	The supporting details are directly connected to the topic.
	The writing is sequenced correctly.
	Resources are acknowledged correctly.
	The conclusion summarizes the information and is directly related to the topic.
	Language mistakes have been corrected.
	There are paragraphs, and they are indented.
	The transitions throughout the writing are used appropriately.
	Handwriting is legible.
	Punctuation and capitalization are used correctly.
	There are spaces between words.
	The non-negotiable words are spelled correctly.
4	All above are checked.
3	Two or three elements are missing, but the piece makes sense.
2	Four or five elements are missing, and the piece doesn't always make sense.
1	Ideas, organization, and conventions all need to be improved.
0	Missing many elements on the list; piece is incomplete.

for all children, the word order, the language used in the prompt, and the structures required to address the prompt are not natural for ELL students, who have different language discourses. Asian children might not address the prompt directly in their writing because they assume the reader will understand what the story is about since the prompt already says it. Latino children will relate stories within stories because their language discourse promotes that. Consequently, writing to prompts is something that not only needs to be taught in class but also needs to be broken down and analyzed in order to be understood.

SUMMARY

When teaching writing to ELL students, it is necessary to teach new language concepts and new discourse, building from background knowledge the students already have. The linguistic and cultural resources teachers can provide to ELL students will determine the level of writing they will achieve. Keep in mind the following when planning for writing instruction:

1. *Build on* students' strengths
   - Encourage students to write about their own experiences
   - Encourage writing in their native language
   - Encourage them to write what they do know in English
   - Encourage students to use drawings or photos to help them structure their ideas and express themselves
2. *Explain*
   - Help solidify and reinforce what students know about how language works
   - Demonstrate to students that you value what they have to say more than perfect writing
   - Make comparisons and connections between how writing in English works and how their native language works
   - Teach students to use the scoring guides to self-monitor their writing
3. *Involve* students by encouraging talk in their native language and English as a bridge to writing in English
   - Provide opportunities for students to rehearse their ideas with one another

- Bring in older students who speak the same language to work with young writers
- Give students opportunities to write with and to you, with and to classmates, and to other audiences
- Involve students in shared and guided writing, encouraging them to talk about what they are writing

4. *Involve* students through the use of native language writing to expand their knowledge of writing
   - When students write in their native language, encourage them to insert known English words where they can
   - Have them share orally in English what they wrote about (ideas, not translation)
   - Express interest in their native language and support their use of English
   - Display and publish their writing for everyone to celebrate

Writing is another way for ELL students to bring together and apply everything they have been learning about how the English language works. In writing, students are helped by speaking about their ideas, listening to what others have to say and listening to how their own written words sound, reading their own and other students' writing, and, of course, getting their ideas down on paper. Throughout this process, ELL students can learn to self-monitor and assess their own language and literacy progress. All aspects of language and literacy come into play during the writing experience, supporting and facilitating ELL students' continued growth toward becoming highly literate individuals.

Conclusion

TEACHING LITERACY TO YOUNG English Language Learners is a privilege; however, it is not an easy task, and it is as much a social phenomenon as it is an academic one. English Language Learners are, in essence, being socialized into the literacy practices of our schools and, at the same time, are expected to perform academically, and meet national standards, in a different culture (Lachat, 2004). The goals for successful literacy development in schools and classrooms include building genuine relationships, establishing mutual trust, and creating high-functioning literacy environments that support a community where children spontaneously engage in thoughtful conversation about books and ideas, ask questions that matter to them, explore their solution, and respond independently to a variety of texts (Miller, 2002).

ELL students come to the classroom from diverse backgrounds, and teachers need to be especially cognizant of their interactions with the new environment. Teachers need to pay attention to how students participate in the school's literacy activities and how they respond to the particular methodologies being used. Simultaneously, teachers will be helping ELL students learn about the details of speaking, reading, and writing in English: vocabulary, grammar, pronunciations, spellings, expressions, punctuation, and more. This means that while the children are learning literacy skills, they also are learning a new language.

Teachers who work with students from diverse linguistic and cultural backgrounds attempt to reach them on an academic level. We have emphasized that, along with academic instruction, the teacher needs to act as a cultural and linguistic mediator by helping students to feel comfortable with their own identities and languages within the school context (Au, 1993; Cappellini, 2005), while at the same time introducing new cultural and linguistic knowledge.

Literacy is not just a matter of reading/writing skills or cognitive strategies; it is also a matter of will, feelings, and emotions. Emotions are highly involved when children attempt to communicate, respond to literature, publish their stories, or share what they learn from their books, because they are sharing a part of themselves (Harvey & Goudvis, 2000). Furthermore, when ELL students perceive reading and writing tasks and materials as reaffirming their cultural identity, they are likely to become more deeply involved and to construct their own personal meanings (Trueba, 1988). On the other hand, if students feel that school literacy tasks and materials deny or devalue their cultural identity, their response is likely to be indifference or resistance (Cappellini, 2005).

The ideal literacy instruction for ELL students uses themes and materials that reaffirm and *build on* students' current knowledge, provides opportunities to create new meanings, and promotes the forging of new understandings and interpersonal relationships along with new language (Peregoy & Boyle, 2005). Teachers need to present reading and writing strategies to students in supportive ways, and with various alternatives, to help them make discoveries and be successful in their new world and with their new language.

Literacy instruction in the classroom should reflect the communicative functions of language and create the kinds of social contexts and conditions in which literacy can and will flourish (Pérez & Torres-Guzmán, 2002). Listening to and expanding upon students' ideas can lead to productive new patterns of instruction. At the same time, ELL students need to learn about the conventional forms and functions of both interpersonal and academic English. In order to learn academic English, students must be given explicit direction and instruction in these new forms and functions (Chamot & O'Malley, 1996; Flynn & Hill, 2006). When teaching ELL students, it is important to understand the differences in their language, literacy, and culture, since the new English forms and functions may or may not be a part of the students' native language repertoire. It is essential to make sure that teaching strategies take advantage of what students do know and build up what they need to know (Pérez & Torres-Guzmán, 2002).

The importance of providing ample opportunities and encouragement *in school* for students to read and write voluminously cannot be overstated (Cummins, 1999; Taberski, 2000). Academic language is the specialized, content-based language found only in books and in school. The English that children need in order to perform according to the standards by which they are challenged is not found on the playground, on the street, or on television. If ELL students are not reading and writing a great deal in school, and doing so in a variety of genres, then they are not getting access to and practice with the language that they need for success (Freeman & Freeman, 2007; Marzano et al., 2004). Academic reading and writing create the path through which students will find academic success.

Guided Reading Instruction

TABLE A.1. Guided Reading Instruction, K–2: Grouping According to Language Proficiency

Instructional Components	Academic Needs	Instructional Strategies
Oral Language Development	Lack of vocabulary Lack of background knowledge and experiences Lack of language structure Difficulty with the level of the text Difficulty with prepositions, conjunctions, and articles Lack of English grammar rules because differ from native language	Implant vocabulary during previewing and reading Use wordless picture books Read aloud and discuss easy books in small groups Use pattern books Use shared reading in small groups Make sure text is at appropriate age level
Phonemic Awareness	Lack of the sounds of English because not in native language Lack of vocabulary in English	Use daily life words Write books using Language Experience Approach Read the environment Collect pictures and photographs; select the sound attribute for each picture; create a sentence with one or two high-frequency word(s) Use familiar songs, chants, poems
Phonics	Limited oral language and lack of vocabulary Inability to use picture cues to figure out how to pronounce a word Absence of structures such as plural noun marker, past tense, present progressive, and so on.	Use pictures to stimulate memory of known words Use wordless picture books to generate text, then write it down Teach decoding by analogy with familiar words Teach sight word development Provide conversations about the properties of words during read aloud
Comprehension	Lack of language discourse, inability to articulate ideas easily Absence of English/U.S. story elements Lack of vocabulary Lack of understanding Low level of language proficiency	Model a retelling (or review what was done during read aloud); make the structure explicit (visuals help) Model summarizing; make the structure explicit (visuals help) Model telling (rather than reading) and retelling a story with the children; make the structure of each explicit (visuals help)

Instructional Components	Academic Needs	Instructional Strategies
Comprehension (continued)		Build vocabulary students can use to help them discuss what they do and don't understand
		Scaffold discussion about the book
		Ask questions often to make sure students are following the thread of the story
		Ask questions to help students make connections to their own lives, other texts, and general knowledge
		Help students make direct connections to their own background knowledge and content instruction
Fluency	Focus on print without considering meaning or English language structure	Model and discuss language structures
	Language overgeneralizations	Build on instruction done in read aloud and shared reading to model language
	Absence of English language structure	Use daily oral language to teach plural, singular, pronouns
	Absence of third person singular verb marker	Review, discuss, teach specific structures of the language
	Absence of possessive noun or pronoun marker	Explain and/or think aloud as you are reading
	Substitution and omission of forms of *to be*	Use language clues so children understand the word
	Either inability to decode unfamiliar words or ability to decode but without meaning	Read sentences with language patterns
		Encourage the use of books on tape
	Lack of comprehension	Record students' reading time, listen with them, and discuss
	Reading speed less than average:	Describe books instead of reading them
	• Second half of 1st grade, 30 words per minute	Reply to child by focusing and reading the sentence without the mistake
	• 2nd grade, 90 words per minute	
Written Responses	Lack of English language	Read aloud often!
	Lack of English structures	Model, model, model
	Being overwhelmed by having ideas and not knowing how to express or write them down	Use shared and guided writing
		Use interactive writing
		Provide sufficient time to write

TABLE A.2. Guided Reading Instruction, Grades 3–5: Grouping According to Language Proficiency

Instructional Components	Academic Needs	Instructional Strategies
Oral Language Development	Lack of vocabulary Lack of background knowledge and experiences Lack of language structure Difficulty with the text Difficulty with prepositions, conjunctions, and articles Lack of English grammar rules because differ from native language Oral language lower than receptive language Lack of knowledge of language patterns	Implant vocabulary during previewing and reading Build on vocabulary developed during read aloud and shared readings Provide a comprehensible text Consider language complexity when choosing a book Work collaboratively (literature circles) Provide time to discuss the book Spend more time on language than structure (pair sharing, get students talking) Draw upon cognates Rely on students' experiences Use written context as a source of oral development Use explanation or the text to develop an understanding of the word instead of giving definitions Teach vocabulary that children will use frequently throughout the day until it becomes part of their own vocabulary Develop language from what they know Teach unknown words that children can use in different contexts, have a potential use, and help them to understand the text Teach words that can be explained using students' vocabulary and that are useful and interesting Associate unknown words with known words During reading, ask students for their favorite word, sentence, or expression Jigsaw the readings: have small groups become experts on parts of the reading, then mix the groups to teach one another Have students complete the story orally

Instructional Components	Academic Needs	Instructional Strategies
Phonemic Awareness and Phonics	Lack of vocabulary	Use daily life words
	Lack of English sounds and letters that are not in native language	Teach decoding by analogy with familiar words
		Teach sight word development
	Inability to use picture cues to figure out how to pronounce a word	Use daily oral language (DOL) activities to focus on identifying sounds and pronouncing them
	Difficulty pronouncing unfamiliar sounds and letters	Teach letters that do not transfer specifically
	Difficulty comprehending unknown words	Use cloze procedure to teach word recognition within context
	Difficulty pronouncing letters that represent unknown speech sounds, e.g., "th" (Spanish speakers)	Teach words by analogy rather than rules
Comprehension: Summarizing vs. Retell	Lack of language discourse, inability to articulate ideas easily	Model a retelling (or review what was done during read aloud); make the structure explicit (visuals help)
	Absence of English/U.S. story elements	Model summarizing; make the structure explicit (visuals help)
	Lack of vocabulary	Model telling (rather than reading) and retelling a story with the children; make the structure of each explicit (visuals help)
	Lack of understanding	
	Low level of language proficiency	
	Difficulty understanding the text	Build vocabulary students can use to discuss what they do and don't understand
	Unfamiliarity with words the author uses	Scaffold discussion about the book
	Lack of background knowledge to understand difficult topic	Provide the language structure
		Provide explicit instruction on patterns of language
	Over-focus on print	Use reading aloud to delve deeper into texts with complex structures and less common vocabulary
	Difficulty interrelating words to understand the text	
	Difficulty with enumeration, time order, compare and contrast, cause and effect, problem/solution	Model questioning and have students generate questions so they learn to think beyond the obvious
		Avoid low-level questions even if the children are struggling
		Remember students' level of cognitive development and ask questions to help them think at a higher level
		Give students a platform to construct deep and critical understanding of the book

Instructional Components	Academic Needs	Instructional Strategies

Fluency	Focus on print without considering meaning or English language structure
	
	Limited view of reading, thinking that it is just about decoding
	
	Ignoring punctuation
	
	Lack of comprehension of the text
	
	Lack of connecting one thought to the next
	
	Insertions, omissions, and mispronunciation of words
	
	Either inability to decode unfamiliar words or ability to decode but without meaning
	
	Lack of intonation that reflects the meaning of the text due to lack of understanding
	
	Reading speed less than average:
	
	  • 3rd grade, 100 words per minute
	
	  • 4th grade, 110 words per minute
	
	  • 5th grade, 120 words per minute
		Use read aloud and shared reading to model fluency
		
		Read aloud in small groups to model language and fluency
		
		Review, discuss, teach specific structures of the language
		
		Encourage the use of books on tape
		
		Tape record students' reading time, listen with them, and discuss
		
		Use Spanish to help connect to reading in English
		
		Provide oral support for readers:
		
		  • Repeated reading
		  • Read naturally
		  • Read through phrasing
		  • Choral reading
		  • Dialogue reading
		  • Call and response
		  • Paired reading
		  • Echo reading
		  • Readers' theater
		
		Use easy books for students to practice oral reading, prepare them to read to younger students

Written Responses	Lack of English language Lack of English structures Lack of vocabulary Lack of understanding the text Lack of background knowledge Being overwhelmed by having ideas and not knowing how to express or write them down	Use books as models for writing Read aloud often Model, model, model Use shared and guided writing Use interactive writing Provide sufficient time to write Pair with older ELL students who have learned to write in English

Instructional Components	Academic Needs	Instructional Strategies
Self-Monitoring	Over-focus on print	Model language structures
	Language generalizations	Use read aloud and shared reading to model language by listening to the sound of the language
	Absence of English language structures, difficulty knowing what "sounds right"	
	Absence of third person singular verb marker	Use DOL to teach plural, singular, pronouns
	Absence of possessive noun or pronoun marker	Teach specific structures of the language and how to listen for them
	Substitution and omission of forms of *to be*	Explain as you are reading
	Overgeneralization of language	Teach students to use language clues so they can self-monitor
	Either inability to decode unfamiliar words or ability to decode but without meaning	Read sentences with different language patterns, work on recognizing differences
	Lack of understanding	Respond to the child by helping to focus and read the sentence without the mistake
	Inability to engage in comprehensible English for daily speech	
	Erroneous grammar patterns, inability to recognize what "sounds right"	
	Lack of understanding of the relationship between meaning and grammar	
	Difficulty seeing the essential meaning of sentence	

References

Amaral, O. M., & Garrison, L. (2002). Helping English learners increase achievement through inquiry-based science instruction. *Bilingual Research Journal, 26*(2), 213–239.

American heritage dictionary of the English language (4th ed.). (2006). Boston: Houghton Mifflin.

Au, K. H. (1993). *Literacy instruction in multicultural settings.* New York: Harcourt Brace College.

Calderon, M. (2006). *Designing and implementing two-way bilingual programs: A step by step guide for administrators, teachers and parents.* Thousand Oaks, CA: Corwin.

Calkins, L. M. (1994). *The art of teaching writing.* Portsmouth, NH: Heinemann.

Cambourne, B. (1995). Toward an educationally relevant theory of literacy learning: Twenty years of inquiry. *The Reading Teacher, 49*(3), 182–190.

Cappellini, M. (2005). *Balancing reading & language learning.* Portland, ME & Newark, DE : Stenhouse & International Reading Association.

Capps, R., Fix, M. E., Murray, J., Ost, J., Passel, J. S., & Herwantoro, S. H. (2005, September). *The new demography of America's schools: Immigration and the No Child Left Behind Act* [Research Report]. Urban Institute. Retrieved December 27, 2007, from http://www.urban.org/publications/311230.html

Center for Research on Education, Diversity, and Excellence (CREDE). (2002). Five standards for effective pedagogy. Retrieved November 29, 2007, from http://crede.berkeley.edu/standards/standards.html

Chamot, A., & O'Malley, M. (1996). The cognitive academic language learning approach: A model for linguistically diverse classrooms [Special issue: The Language-Minority Student in Transition]. *The Elementary School Journal, 96*(3), 259–273.

Chen, L., & Mora-Flores, E. (2006). *Balanced literacy for English language learners, K–2.* Portsmouth, NH: Heinemann.

Chukovsky, K. (1963). *From two to five.* Berkeley: University of California Press.

Cummins, J. (1981). The role of primary language development in promoting educational success for language minority students. In *Schooling and language minority students* (pp. 3–49). Sacramento: California Department of Education.

Cummins, J. (1999, April). *Building English proficiency among ESL students.* Paper presented at the Accelerating Second Language and Literacy Development Conference, Denver, CO.

Diller, D. (2007). *Making the most of small groups: Differentiation for all.* Portland, ME: Stenhouse.

Dutro, S., & Moran, C. (2003). Rethinking English language instruction: An architectural approach. In G. A. Garcia (Ed.), *English learners: Reaching the highest level of English literacy* (pp. 227–258). Newark, DE: International Reading Association.

Echevarria, J., & Graves, A. (2003). *Sheltered content instruction* (2nd ed.). New York: Pearson Education.

Echevarria, J., Vogt, M., & Short, D. (2004). *Making content comprehensible for English language learners* (2nd ed.). Boston: Allyn & Bacon.

Elementary Science Integration Project. (n.d.). Retrieved January 7, 2008, from http://www.esiponline.org/classroom/foundations/reading/readalouds.html

Escamilla, K. (1993). Promoting biliteracy. In J. Tinajero & A. Flor Ada (Eds.), *The power of two languages: Literacy and biliteracy for Spanish speaking children* (pp. 220–233). New York: McMillan/McGraw-Hill.

Escamilla, K. (1999). Teaching literacy in Spanish. In R. Devillar & J. Tinajero (Eds.), *The power of two languages, 2000* (pp. 126–141). New York: McMillan/McGraw-Hill.

Escamilla, K., & Coady, M. (2001). Assessing the writing of Spanish-speaking students: Issues and suggestions. In J. Tinajero & S. Hurley (Eds.), *Handbook for literacy assessment for bilingual learners* (pp. 43–63). Boston: Allyn & Bacon.

Flynn, K., & Hill, J. (2006). *Classroom instruction that works with English language learners.* Alexandria, VA: Association for Supervision and Curriculum Development.

Fountas, I., & Pinnell, G. (2001). *Guiding readers and writers: Grades 3–6.* Portsmouth, NH: Heinemann.

Freeman, D. E., & Freeman, Y. S. (2004). *Essential linguistics: What you need to know to teach reading, ESL, spelling, phonics, grammar.* Portsmouth, NH: Heinemann.

Freeman, D., & Freeman, Y. (2007). *English language learners: The essential guide.* New York: Scholastic.

Gibbons, P. (1991). *Learning to learn in a second language.* Newton, Australia: Primary English Teaching Association.

Gibbons, P. (2002). *Scaffolding language, scaffolding learning: Teaching second language learners in the mainstream classroom.* Portsmouth, NH: Heinemann.

González, N., Moll, L. C., & Amanti, C. (2005). *Funds of knowledge: Theorizing practices in households and classrooms.* Mahwah, NJ: Erlbaum.

Goodman, Y., & Wilde, S. (Eds.). (1992). *Literacy events in a community of young writers.* New York: Teachers College Press.

Gottlieb, M. (2006). *Assessing English language learners.* Thousand Oaks, CA: Corwin.

Graves, D. (1989). *Investigating non fiction.* Portsmouth, NH: Heinemann.

Guasti, M. T. (2004). *Language acquisition: The growth of grammar.* Cambridge, MA: MIT Press.

Halliday, M.A.K. (1975). *Learning how to mean: Explorations in the development of language.* London: Arnold.

Harklau, L. (1999). Representing culture in the ESL writing classroom. In E. Hinkel (Ed.), *Culture in second language learning and teaching* (pp. 109–135). New York: Cambridge University Press.

Harvey, S., & Goudvis, A. (2000). *Strategies that work.* York, ME: Stenhouse.

Holdaway, D. (1979). *The foundations of literacy.* Sydney, Australia: Ashton Books.

Houk, F. A. (2005). *Supporting English language learners.* Portsmouth, NH: Heinemann.

Jiménez, A.F.J. (2004). A sociocultural approach for language attrition. In M. S. Schmid, B. Kopke, M. Keijzer, & L. Weilemar (Eds.), *First language attrition: Interdisciplinary perspectives on methodological issues* (pp. 61–80). Philadelphia: John Benjamins.

Keene, E., & Zimmermann, S. (2007). *Mosaic of thought: Teaching comprehension in a reader's workshop* (2nd ed.). Portsmouth, NH: Heinemann.

Kendal, J., & Khuon, O. (2005). *Making sense: Small group comprehension lessons.* Portland, ME: Stenhouse.

Kendal, J., & Khuon, O. (2006). *Writing sense: Integrating reading and writing lessons for English language learners.* Portland, ME: Stenhouse.

Krashen, S. (1981). *Second language acquisition and second language learning.* London: Pergamon.

Krashen, S. (2004). *The power of reading* (2nd ed.). Portsmouth, NH: Heinemann.

Lachat, M. A. (2004). *Standards-based instruction and assessments for English language learners.* Thousand Oaks, CA: Corwin.

Marzano, R. J., Pickering, D. J., & Pollock, J. E. (2004). *Classroom instruction that works: Research-based strategies for increasing student achievement.* Alexandria, VA: Association for Supervision and Curriculum Development.

Miller, D. (2002). *Reading with meaning.* Portland, ME: Stenhouse.

Moje, E. B., Ciechanowski, K. M., Kramer, K., Ellis, L., Carrillo, R., & Collazo, T. (2004). Working toward third space in content area literacy: An examination of everyday funds of knowledge and discourse. *Reading Research Quarterly, 39*(1), 38–69.

Nathenson-Mejía, S. (1989). Writing in a second language: Negotiating meaning through invented spelling. *Language Arts, 66*(5), 516–526.

Nathenson-Mejía, S. (1992). Helping young writers working in Spanish: Informing instruction through analysis of writing in Spanish. *Bilingual Research Journal, 16*(3 & 4), 53–67.

National Clearinghouse for English Language Acquisition and Language Instruction Educational Programs. (2007). National and regional data and demographics. Retrieved April 7, 2008, from http://www.ncela.gwu.edu/stats/2_nation.htm

National Council of Teachers of English/International Reading Association. (1996). Standards for the English language arts. Retrieved April 7, 2008, from http://www.ncte.org/about/over/standards/110846.htm

National Reading Panel. (2000). About the National Reading Panel. Retrieved November 29, 2007, from http://www.nationalreadingpanel.org/NRPAbout/about_nrp.htm

Nelson, N. W. (1998). *Childhood language disorders in context.* Boston: Allyn & Bacon.

North West Regional Education Laboratory. (2007). The National Reading Panel: Five components of reading instruction: Frequently asked questions. Retrieved November 29, 2007, from http://www.nwrel.org/learns/resources/toolkit/NationalReadingPanel_FAQ.pdf

Ovando, C. J., Collier, V. P., & Combs, M. C. (2003). *Bilingual and ESL classrooms: Teaching in multicultural contexts* (3rd ed.). Boston: McGraw-Hill.

Pearson, P. D. (1976). A psycholinguistic model of reading. *Language Arts, 53,* 309–314.

Peregoy, S., & Boyle, F. (2008). *Reading, writing, and learning in ESL* (5th ed.). Boston: Allyn & Bacon.

Pérez, B., & Torres-Guzmán, M. (2002). *Learning in two worlds* (3rd ed.). Boston: Allyn & Bacon.

Piaget, J., & Inhelder, B. (1969). *The psychology of the child*. New York: Basic Books.

Raphael, T. E. (1986). Teaching question answer relationships, revisited. *Reading Teacher, 39*(6), 516–522.

Raphael, T. E., Highfield, K., & Au, K. H. (2006). *QAR now: A powerful and practical framework that develops comprehension and higher-level thinking in all students*. New York: Scholastic.

Reeves, D. (2003a). *Accountability in action*. Denver, CO: Lead & Learn.

Reeves, D. (2003b). *Making standards work*. Englewood, CO: ALP.

Richardson, J. (2004, January). Guided reading. Presentation at a Denver Public Schools inservice program. Denver, CO.

Routman, R. (1994). *Invitations*. Portsmouth, NH: Heinemann.

Schutz, R. (2004). *Vygotsky and language acquisition*. Retrieved September 30, 2007, from http://www.sj.com.br/sk-vygot.html

Short, D., & Fitzsimmons, S. (2007). *Double the work: Challenges and solutions to acquiring language and academic literacy for adolescent English language learners—A report to Carnegie Corporation of New York*. Washington, DC: Alliance for Excellent Education.

Smiley, P., & Salsberry, T. (2007). *Effective schooling for English language learners: What elementary principals should know and do*. Poughkeepsie, NY: Eye On Education.

Stead, T. (2001). *Is that a fact? Teaching nonfiction writing K–3*. Portland, ME: Stenhouse.

Taberski, S. (2000). *On solid ground*. Portsmouth, NH: Heinemann.

Taverna, P., & Hongell, T. (2005). *Vietnam: A children's guide*. Retrieved October 30, 2007, from http://www.pocanticohills.org/vietnam/know.htm

Trueba, H. (1988). Culturally based explanations of minority students' academic achievement. *Anthology and Education Quarterly, 19*(3), 270–287.

Uribe, M. (2004). Effective literacy instruction. Unpublished dissertation, University of Colorado at Denver.

Venturini, M., & Uribe, M. (2003). *Sounds from English and their relationship to Spanish*. Denver, CO: Denver Public Schools.

Vygotsky, L. (1986). *Thought and language* (Rev. ed.). Cumberland, RI: MIT Press.

Walsh, J. A., & Sattes, B. D. (2004). *Quality questioning: Research based practice to engage every learner*. Thousand Oaks, CA: Corwin.

Weaver, C. (2002). *Reading process & practice* (3rd ed.). Portsmouth, NH: Heinemann.

Wong-Fillmore, L., & Snow, C. (2000). What teachers need to know about language. Retrieved November 29, 2007, from http://faculty.tamu-commerce.edu/jthompson/Resources/FillmoreSnow2000.pdf

Children's Literature Cited

Ackerman, K. (1988). *Song and dance man*. New York: Knopf. Illustrated by Stephen Gammell.

Adler, D. (1989). *Malke's secret recipe*. Rockville, MD: Kar-Ben Copies.

Baer, E. (1990). *This is the way we go to school*. Topeka, KS: Tandem Library Books. Illustrated by Steve Bjorkman.

Baylor, B. (1974). *Everybody needs a rock*. New York: Aladdin. Illustrated by Peter Parnall.

Brown, M. (2005). *Stone soup*. New York: Aladdin.

Carle, E. (2005). *Pancakes, pancakes*. New York: Aladdin/Simon & Schuster.

dePaola, T. (1978). *Pancakes for breakfast*. New York: Voyager/Harcourt Brace Jovanovich.

Doering, A. (2005). *Homes around the world ABC: An alphabet book*. Manketo, MN: Capstone.

Dorros, A. (1992). *This is my house*. New York: Scholastic.

Freeman, D. (2003). *How people live*. New York: DK Publishers.

Goble, P. (1980). *The gift of the sacred dog*. New York: Bradbury.

Johnston, T. (1985). *The quilt story*. New York: Scholastic. Illustrated by Tomie dePaola.

Kasza, K. (1987). *Wolf's chicken stew*. New York: Trumpet Club.

Look, L. (1999). *Love as strong as ginger*. New York: Atheneum. Illustrated by Stephen T. Johnson.

Lorbiecki, M. (1998). *Sister Anne's hands*. New York: Puffin. Illustrated by K. Wendy Popp.

Lowell, S. (1992). *The three little javelinas*. Flagstaff, AZ: Rising Moon.

Menzel, P. (1995). *Material world: A global family portrait*. San Francisco: Sierra Club.

Morris, A. (1992). *Houses and homes*. New York: HarperCollins. Illustrated by Ken Heyman.

Nelson, V. M. (2003). *Almost to freedom*. New York: Scholastic. Illustrated by Colin Bootman.

Nolen, J. (2001). *In my momma's kitchen*. New York: Amistad. Illustrated by Colin Bootman.

Nye, N. S. (1994). *Sitti's secrets*. New York: Aladdin. Illustrated by Nancy Carpenter.

Polacco, P. (1990). *Thundercake*. New York: Philomel.

Polacco, P. (1992). *Mrs. Katz and Tush*. New York: Dell.

Say, A. (1993). *Grandfather's journey*. New York: Houghton Mifflin.

Scieszka, J. (1996). *The true story of the 3 little pigs*. New York: Puffin. Illustrated by Lane Smith.

Stevens, J., & Crummel, S. S. (1999). *Cock-a-doodle-doo!* New York: Harcourt Brace. Illustrated by Janet Stevens.

Torres, L. (1995). *Saturday sancocho*. New York: Farrar Straus Giroux.

van Hichtum, N. (1996). *The apple cake*. Edinburgh, Scotland: Floris.

Weston, T. (2003). *Hey, pancakes!* San Diego, CA: Harcourt. Illustrated by Stephen Gammell.

Williams, V. B. (1982). *A chair for my mother*. New York: Scholastic.

Index

About the Authors

Maria Uribe is the principal of Goldrick Elementary, an urban school in Denver, Colorado. She also works as an adjunct professor at the University of Colorado Denver. Maria began her teaching career in her native country, Colombia, South America, where she taught for 13 years in bilingual schools. After moving to Denver, Maria taught 1st grade at Goldrick for 9 years and was then a coach and the teacher licensing program's site coordinator for UCD for 7 years. She has received various recognitions, including the Colorado Association of Bilingual Education president's award in 2007. She has published a number of articles on bilingual education and second language learners. Maria designed the bilingual program at her school and has worked with Dr. Sally Nathenson-Mejía presenting workshops about literacy strategies for English Language Learners. Maria earned a master's degree in Multicultural and Bilingual Education from the University of Colorado at Boulder and a Ph.D. from the University of Colorado Denver.

Sally Nathenson-Mejía is an associate professor in the School of Education and Human Development at the University of Colorado Denver. Through her teaching and research for the past 25 years, Sally has been involved with elementary and secondary teachers who work with English Language Learners. Her teaching career began in Minnesota, but she soon moved to Puebla, Mexico, where she taught elementary school. Sally's research and publications focus on understanding the literacy development of children as they become bilingual and biliterate and on how to help urban teachers understand the wealth of background English Language Learners bring to the classroom. Together with Dr. Maria Uribe, Sally has presented workshops and inservices on literacy to teachers around the greater Denver metro area. She earned her master's and doctoral degrees in Reading/Writing, Multicultural and Bilingual Education from The Ohio State University.